# Pennsylvania:

## The German Influence in Its Settlement and Development

A Narrative and Critical History

---

### Part V

The German Emigration From New York Province into Pennsylvania

By:

Rev. Matthias Henry Richards, D.D.

# Notice

In many older books, foxing (or discoloration) occurs and, in some instances, print lightens with wear and age. Reprinted books, such as this, often duplicate these flaws, notwithstanding efforts to reduce or eliminate them. The pages of this reprint have been digitally enhanced and, where possible, the flaws eliminated in order to provide clarity of content and a pleasant reading experience.

Excerpted from:

*Pennsylvania: The German Influence in Its Settlement and Development – A Narrative and Critical History.* Part V, Pages 351-447. Originally published Lancaster, Pennsylvania, 1899.

Reprinted:

Janaway Publishing, Inc.
2412 Nicklaus Dr.
Santa Maria, California 93455
(805) 925-1038
www.janawaygenealogy.com

2006

ISBN 10: 1-59641-019-1
ISBN 13: 978-1-59641-019-0

*Made in the United States of America*

# Publisher's Preface

This book has been excerpted from *Pennsylvania: The German Influence in Its Settlement and Development – A Narrative and Critical History,* Part V, which was originally published in Lancaster, Pennsylvania, 1899, and includes pages 351 to 447 of the original volume. This work retains those original page numbers.

Janaway Publishing, Inc.

## CHAPTER I.

## THE GERMAN EMIGRATION FROM NEW YORK PROVINCE INTO PENNSYLVANIA.

PRELIMINARY RESUMÉ.[1]

THE task assigned to me is to present the features of what may, in some respects, be called an episode of that migration of Palatines which took place in 1710, and which sought its hoped for resting place in New York Province, only to find the rather a prison house and a land of bondage. In other respects, this subsequent migration to Pennsylvania, though scanty as to numbers, was influential to no inconsiderable degree and deserves therefore a consideration far beyond that which should be accorded

---

[1] The sudden decease of the Rev. Dr. M. H. Richards, on Dec. 12, 1898, left his paper in an unfinished condition. At the request of the Executive Committee of the Pennsylvania-German Society the work of amplification and completion has been reluctantly undertaken by his brother, Henry Melchior Muhlenberg Richards.

otherwise to it in proportion to its extent. Why these Palatines were moved to migration, how that migration took place, whither it was directed, and in what it ended, are all matters which have been treated most adequately already. They formed the contents of an able and carefully prepared paper read before this body at its last annual meeting. But it is pardonable, perhaps desirable, to set forth these things once more, as in a summary, in order to introduce satisfactorily the contents of this present paper.

Be it recalled then that the Palatinate had been the seat of cruel and wasteful warfare, had been devastated in 1683, and again in 1693. Its future was as dark as its present was wretched. Religious persecution went hand in hand with material misery. Even nature seemed to have doomed the land, when, in the winter of 1709, the cold became so intense that birds fell dead from it in the midst of their flight, and wild beasts perished in their hiding-places. At the same time the fame of America as a land of promise and plenty began to be spread abroad. It was declared that Queen Anne, of England, stood ready to give a free passage to the forlorn, impoverished, persecuted Palatines, if they saw fit to embark for her colonies in that new land. A yearning resolve, such as marked the Crusades, spread like a pestilence, until a mass-migration ensued; and 14,000 Palatines and inhabitants of territory contiguous to the Palatinate stood upon the shores of Eng-

Seal of the Province of New York.

land, in the neighborhood of London, asking and expecting help, homes, food for present need. Even royal charity and willingness was confounded. But every effort was made, and gradually these unfortunates, or their survivors rather, were located here and there, notably in Ireland and America.

Five Indian chiefs, constituting an embassage to the British Government, witnessed the misery of this encampment of exiles, and pitied them so greatly as to offer to open for their settlement part of the lands under their control. This offer led to the migration, under the royal charge, of 4,000 to the Province of New York, these Palatines expecting an assignment of land, under this Indian promise, and hopeful that industry and peace would restore them to prosperity and happiness. But the governor of the Province, Robert Hunter, along with a wealthy proprietor therein, Robert Livingston, had planned their own profit out of the bondage of these strangers. Demands and charges and unexpected conditions fell upon them in their settlement upon the Hudson which, if submitted unto, reduced them to serfdom. It had been as well to have died at home as to suffer and die here! Again the hope and courage of better things came to them, and they took their flight, in large number, to the Mohawk lands, the consent of the Indians having been gained to their entrance upon them, according to the promise made in England. In the Spring of 1714 we find 150 families around Schoharie, forty miles from Albany. Here they toiled and starved until it was possible, by another year, to prepare ground enough for the sowing of grain and planting of corn for their sustenence. At last they have found rest! No, not even yet! They have no title to their land, save from their Indian friends. The governor of the Province sells this land, valueless except for what their labor has done for it, unopen to settlement, save as Indian pity had opened it for them, to other provincials as greedy and pitiless as himself, and invokes the power of the State against these still unhappy Palatines! Then arose threats of armed resistance, the actual sending of three deputies to England to present their case to the Throne, the usual ineffectual outcome when helplessness is worried out by the law's delays and thwarted by the insolence of office. In 1723 affairs stood thus: Hunter had lost his office, a royal order instructed William Burnet, the new governor, to assign *vacant* lands to all the Germans who had been sent to New York under the late Queen. The new governor did willingly what he could, but "vacant lands" would not mean the retention of what rightfully belonged to these Palatines. The result was various: Some acquiesced, some went to other locations in the Province, and some determined to migrate once more, and this time to Penn's Province of Pennsylvania. It is our duty to follow the experiences and fortunes of these, since these form the migration from New York Province into Pennsylvania.

## CHAPTER II.

### The Minisink Settlement.

WE are so accustomed to trace the history of Pennsylvania from its beginnings at and below Philadelphia that we overlook a fact but little known to the general public, which is the Minisink Settlement along the banks of the Delaware, above the present town of Stroudsburg in Monroe County. There is a romance surrounding its existence, shrouded as it is in mystery, most inviting to the historian, but, as yet, the veil has not been fully lifted. From what is known concerning it there seems to be but little doubt that it is the oldest European settlement in Pennsylvania, antedating the advent of Penn in 1682. For years its people lived, toiled, married, suffered, were happy and died in a world of their own, unknown to those who planted their feet, somewhat later, on the banks of the same river so many miles to the south of them. At peace with their neighbor, the Indian, from whom their lands had been fairly purchased, they little dreamed of the danger which threatened them from a government of whose existence, even, they were utterly oblivious.

This state of affairs could not exist forever. About 1720 the English authorities had been informed with regard to the settlement, and in 1729 a law was passed that any such purchases made from the Indians should be void, and the purchasers indicted for "forcible entry and detainer," according to the laws of England. Prior to that, in 1727, the famous surveyor, Nicholas Scull, was directed to go and investigate the facts. Accompanied by Matthew Hughes, a Justice of the Peace from Bucks County, with two others, one being his apprentice, Mr. John Lukens, and hired Indian guides, after a fatiguing journey, through what was then a wilderness uninhabited by any but aborigines, Mr. Scull finally reached his destination. The astonishment of the party was great at the sight which met their eyes. On all hands were to be seen cultivated fields and well established homes. Everywhere were thriving orchards and groves of apple trees, of a size and age far beyond any at Philadelphia. The people who inhabited these fertile flats were mostly Hollanders, whose ancestors had come from New York Province and who had never even heard of William Penn, his city of Brotherly Love or his Proprietary Government.

With a laudable curiosity to know more about the origin of these strange people Mr. Lukens asked them many questions, and, in later years (1787), at his instigation, Mr. Samuel Preston, of Stockport, Wayne County, made a special tour of investigation to the same locality. The result was by no mean conclusive and only elicited the fact that the original settlers were, generally, the grandparents of those residing there in 1787, who were, at the time they gave the information, themselves old men. Their communication with the outer world was over a well defined road leading to Esopus, now Kingston, N. Y., which, in former years, had been opened up, with great labor, to give access to two mines, one on the Delaware, where the mountain nearly approaches the lower point of Paaquarry flat, the other at the north foot of the same mountain near half-way between the Delaware and Esopus. Indeed so much labor had been expended in the construction of this road, nearly 100 miles long, that it was supposed the Dutch authorities themselves had aided in its building before the advent of the English in 1664. Its primary object, however, was for mining purposes, and many tons of ore are said to have been hauled over it to Esopus. That such was a fact was evidenced by the appearance of the old mine holes, then visited, but the nature of the ore could never be ascertained.

An Old Dutch Home in New York.

As the miners traversed its length, back and forth, they were struck with the extreme fertility of the Minisink Flats, and were, doubtless, led to select this place for their homes when their countrymen had been displaced by the foreign English power and, to all intents and purposes, an end put to their business of mining.

Whilst it is true these men were Hollanders, or, at least, are so called, and no claims can be made that the settlement was of German origin, yet, outside of its general interest as, probably, the oldest white settlement in the Province, and outside of the further interesting fact that its people migrated thence from New York, it is by no means devoid of bearing and value in connection with our subject now under consideration.

In the first place these settlers, whilst generally from Holland, were not all so. Even the meager data in our hands show that amongst them were persons of French and Spanish nationality. May there not have been also some from Germany? Of still more interest, however, is the fact that, whilst mining and the transportation of ore did cease, yet intercourse with Esopus did not. This was their market. Without knowledge of Philadelphia, and not knowing whence ran the stream which flowed before their doors, every winter, with loads of wheat and cider, they wended their way over the old Mine Road to Esopus, to return with salt and such necessaries with which they could not provide themselves. Situated as was this town, in close proximity to the Livingston Manor, in time the settlers must have come into intercourse with the German Palatines who were located all around it. Who can tell what tales of peace, prosperity and happiness were poured by the Pennsylvania settlers, who had little reason to love the English, into the ears of their German brethren still sighing for freedom under their own roof, the pursuit of which drove them from the Fatherland and the attainment of which seemed to ever elude their grasp? It is but natural to suppose that some information was gained, and it can hardly be doubted but that this fact had somewhat to do with the immigration from New York Province into Pennsylvania which followed.

This leads us then to a consideration of the reasons and influences which diverted the German immigration to an entirely different path into Penn's Province.

## CHAPTER III.

### The Choice of a Home.

MERELY because the Germans were of another nationality we can understand why there should be no enthusiastic desire to commingle with their Dutch brethren, but, beyond all this, the time had not yet arrived when the thought of immigration in that direction had come to maturity. For a while they clung to the hope of a happy issue from their troubles at Livingston Manor itself. When this was no longer possible and, as outcasts, they were forced, once more, to take up the struggle for a home, it was but natural they should remember the lands promised them by their Indian friends in London, and to wend their way towards Schoharie rather than towards the hunting grounds of a hostile tribe. Still, it may even be that some Germans then commingled with the Dutch on the Minisink Flats, but of that we have no evidence whatever, save the existence of a few German names which may have come in later, and, indeed, from other parts of the same Province. It was only when driven from their new homes up the Hudson, that to many came the determination to quit forever the land in which they had experienced so many trials and so much misery. Then did they remember all they had heard of that land of promise, Pennsylvania, and, with it as their goal, it only remained to decide upon the precise point of location.

How few persons are aware that a most trifling fact alone prevented the Palatines from making their homes on or near the Minisink Flats, at this point in their history. "Man proposes and God disposes," and the all-wise Father had a different destination selected and a different destiny in view for the heretofore despised Germans who were to mould the future of a great State after first saving its life.

When the last and most severe blow fell on those at Schoharie there seemed but one resort left to them, the appeal to the Throne, and we are familiar with the story of their selection of delegates, of the hardships experienced by those delegates on their voyage to England, and of all their trials upon arrival, during the weary years of waiting for a verdict. We are by no means familiar, however, with the fact that John Conrad Weiser, the principal one of these delegates, having in mind all he had heard at Esopus of the fertile Minisink low lands along the banks of the Upper Delaware, visited the widow of William Penn, at her home in Ruscombe, Berkshire, also interviewed members of the family, notably John Penn, either there or in London, and endeavored to arrange with them for the purchase of lands contiguous to the Dutch settlement. He by no means met with rebuff, and, it is most certain, would have been entirely successful, but, apparently, for the desire of James Logan, the Provincial Secretary, to ac-

## Secretary Logan's Interference.

quire the greatest possible amount of money for the Proprietors.

Amongst the " Papers Relating to Provincial Affairs" is a letter from James Logan to John Penn, dated Philad'a, 25th Nov'r, 1727. The following extract from it tells the story. Speaking of the division of the property amongst the heirs he says:

"About William's Share, which thou particularly recommends, I have been anxious, but there are certain rich low Lands on Delaware, near a hund$^d$ miles northward on a Streight Line, not far from a Dutch settlem$^t$, at a place called Mackhackomack in Jersey, and on the confines of N. York Governm$^t$, w$^{ch}$ settlem$^t$ is about 50 miles from Kingston or Esopus, on Hudson's River. A certain German of the Palatinate, named Conradt Wyser, who was with thee at Ruscomb or London in the year 1723, treating about Lands, recv'd a few Lines from thee at Lond. wrote from Ruscomb, w$^{ch}$ only shew that you had talk'd together about somewhat, but mention not so much as the word Land. A friend of his also made affidavit about some words that pass'd between the Mother and Wyser concerning Land here. From these, that fellow has had the assurance to pretend a power from you to Sell Lands, and thereupon made an agreem$^t$ with several People for parcels of those rich Tracts I have mentioned, upon which they have proceeded to purchase Rights of the Indians at excessive prices. Being informed of this, I did what lay in my power to make the People sensible of the cheat, that their Purchases of the Indians were against our Laws, and that their agreemen$^t$ with Wyser was of no validity. One J. Crook, of Kingston, in N. York Governm$^t$, has wrote to thee about these Lands, but having no answer, he endeavored to take a shorter method, w$^{ch}$ was to purchase in

THE PENNSYLVANIA-GERMAN SOCIETY.

this town old unlocated Original Rights from thy father's sales in Engl$^d$, by Lease & Release, with a design to lay these on such parcels as they have paid for to the Indians. We, the Trustees, coming about ten days since to the knowledge of this, to prevent, as far as we could, such irregular practices, resolved to lay thy Nephew William's Right on these Lands, and have actually sent up the Surveyor Gen$^l$, with two others, accompanied with one Matthew Hughes, a Justice of the Peace for Bucks County, a magistrate's presence being necessary, and they are now in most unpleasant, severe weather upon the business, from w$^{ch}$ I wish they may return alive & in any tolerable state of health, for they have high, rugged mountains and some deep waters to pass, without any Road or Inhabitants, some good part of the way. There is not above 2 or 3 thous$^d$ acres (they say) of that rich Land, and the adjoining is all Rocks & Hills; yet as it is not above 60 miles or thereabouts from Hudson's River, the Dutch People of N. York Governm$^t$ sett a very great value upon it, and were it clear from Indian Claims, would sell readily for good Pay and at a high rate, perhaps 60 or 70$^{lbs}$ p. 100 acres, if not more. These Bottoms, I mean, for the rest is good for nothing. I wish we may gett the Survey compleated without any opposition from the Indians, for w$^{ch}$ I have taken all possible precautions, and then these Lands will be William's for so we shall return them. . . . ."

In addition to the above the following letter was previously sent Weiser:

Philad$^{ia}$, 8$^{th}$ June, 1727.

CONRAD WEISER:

*Sir:* Being informed not only of thy settling our Prop$^{tr}$ Lands on y$^e$ River Delaware, but of thy undertaking to sell them to others on pretense of our authority so to doe, I could not at first give any credit to the story till it was afterwards, to my very great surprise, confirmed by several hands. I remember either thy self, or somebody for thee, shew$^d$ me, at my house, a few Lines from John Penn, directed, as I remember, to one of the Trustees of this Province, recommending thee to him to make some agreem$^t$ with thee, or at least to give thee some encouragem$^t$. But sure I am that no agreem$^t$ was ever made with thee, nor any Power ever given thee, by w$^{ch}$ thou canst justify thy Proceedings. Therefore, Pray lett common sense and Honesty so far prevail with thee as to forbear imposing on any others under those frivolous pretences, otherwise all that are concerned with thee as thy self may assure yourselves that you must suffer for your Trespasses. If thou makes a proper use of this Lette$^r$ (of w$^{ch}$ I have given a copy to be shown to those who deal with thee) it may prevent further trouble and confusion, which is the real desire of

                 Thy well wishing friend
                           J. LOGAN.

Cut off from the hope of settlement on the Delaware, when Weiser reached Schoharie again he could only recommend one route to those who desired to enter Pennsylvania, that by the Susquehanna River.

A glance at the map will show that the head waters of this river rise in New York, not very remotely from the Schoharie Valley. When once attained the emigrants could float down its waters to their new home. Nor would they attract attention or run any danger of arrest, in so doing, from the authorities of the Province. They were beyond the line of settlement and were entering into that part of Pennsylvania which was equally unsettled. They must take up vacant lands whither they were going, and this would, indeed, be a direct course to such a section.

But outside of geographical considerations, which shut up the wanderers to their course down the Susquehanna, there had not been lacking broad intimations, if not positive invitations and promises from the government of Pennsylvania, which were rendered all the more attractive by the well-earned reputation of William Penn for generous treatment and mild laws. Pennsylvania was not unknown to the Germans. There was the "Frankfort Land Company," incorporated 1686, whose possessions were at Germantown, and the "Manatawney Patent"—thousands of acres—whose attorney in 1708 was Daniel Falkner. Of the Palatines, from 1708-20, very many came directly to Pennsylvania. They continued coming for many years after this, until the authorities began to fear that the Province would cease to be English, or respect English authority. There are not lacking rumors that Sir William Keith, while governor of the colony, had schemes of founding an independent colony towards the Ohio, and was so friendly toward the Palatines with an eye to this brilliant scheme. At all events it remains a fact that this William Keith was visiting in Albany at the time of the distress of the Palatines and gave them encouragement to come to his colony. In keeping with this is the following petition addressed to him by our immigrants shortly after their settlement in his Province.[2]

"To his Excellency, William Keith, Baronet, Governor of Pennsylvania, &c., &c., the Honorable Council.

"The petition of us, the subscribers, being thirty-three

---

[2] See Col. Records, Vol. 3, p. 341.

families in number, at present inhabiting Tulpehocken Creek.

"HUMBLY SHEWETH,

"That your petitioners being natives of Germany, about fifteen years ago, were by the great goodness and royal bounty of her late Majesty, Queen Anne, relieved from the hardships which they then suffered in Europe, and were transported into the colony of New York, where they settled. But their families increasing, being in that Government confined to the scanty allowance of ten acres of land to each family, whereon they could not well subsist. Your petitioners being informed of the kind reception which their countrymen usually meet with in the Province of Pennsylvania, and hoping they might, with what substance they had, acquire larger settlements in that Province, did last year (in the spring of 1723), leave their settlements in New York Government, and come with their families into this province, where, upon their arrival, they applied themselves to His Excellency, the Governor, who, of his great goodness, permitted them to inhabit upon Tulpehaca Creek (being the farthest inhabited part of the province northwest of Philadelphia), on condition that they should make full satisfaction to the proprietor or his agents, for such lands as should be allotted to them, when they were ready to receive the same. And now, your petitioners, understanding that some gentlemen, agents of the proprietor, have ample power to dispose of lands in this province. And we, your petitioners, being willing and ready to purchase, do humbly beseech your Excellency and council to recommend us to the favorable usage of the proprietor's agents, that upon paying the usual prices for lands at such distance from Philadelphia, we may have sufficient rights and titles made to us for such lands as we shall have occasion to buy, that our children may have some settlement to depend on hereafter, and that by your authority we may be freed from the demands of the Indians of that part of the country, who pretend a right thereto. And we humbly beg leave to inform your Excellency and Council, that there are fifty families more who, if they may be admitted upon the same conditions, are desirous to come and settle with us. We hope for your favorable answer to this our humble request, and as in duty bound shall ever pray, &c."

Johannes Yans            Johannes Claes Shaver
Peter Ritt               Jo. Hamelar Ritt
Conrad Schitz            Antonis Sharb
Paltus Unsf              Johan Peter Pacht
Toritine Serbo           Jocham Michael Cricht
Josap Sab                Sebastian Pisas
Jorge Ritt               Andrew Falborn
            Godfreyt Filler.[3]

---

[3] The names to the petition, being mostly in a deep German hand, could not be read, but by one skilled in German writing (which is decidedly manifest). They are given as above.

## CHAPTER IV.

### The Emigration to Pennsylvania.

Wurtemberg.

THE place and route decided it remained but to put their project into execution. In the spring of 1723 a certain number of families, not exceeding thirty-three, the names of many of whose heads we have just read, turned their backs on those with whom they had experienced so many trials and sufferings in the past and so few joys, and turned their faces towards the setting sun as it sank below the unknown wilderness which lay before them with all its hidden dangers.

There is something not only pathetic, but grand and noble, in the stalwart faith of these people which led them to this act, far exceeding, in romance and daring, any parallel performance in the history of this land. What was the deed of either Puritan or Cavalier, so constantly on the lips of everyone, compared to that of these despised and down-trodden Germans? They too endured persecution in the home land for religion's sake, but they endured it patiently for a century until home, land and, often, family was gone and neither endurance nor patience was any longer a virtue. They too endured the horrors of the terrible voyage across the Atlantic, but when they landed their feet did not rest on the shores of Freedom; their coming was only to another slavery. And now, unlike the Pilgrims or any other of the peoples who came to this country, they alone once more resolutely set out to seek a home where they may peacefully live and worship their God in accordance with the dictates of their conscience, knowing full well the great dangers which lay before them, dangers apparently greater than any experienced in the past.

It is difficult for us, of our day, to fully imagine the trackless wilderness which literally covered the territory now teeming with cities, cultivated farms and civilized life of every description. One immense forest practically extended from Schoharie to their destination on the head waters of the Susquehanna, through which alone roamed the wild beast and still wilder savage man. The river gained, its waters floated them, day by day, through a desolate country, without sign of habitation or habitant. How interesting to us could we but picture them to ourselves, mentally, on their daily journey, and what a revelation to them could the future of the noble stream, on whose bosom they were borne, have been spread before them!

Guided by the Indians, and not under the leadership of either the elder Weiser, or his gifted son, as some suppose, both of whom came later, the pioneers of 1723, with much toil and labor, cut their way through the forest, after which, with their wives, little ones and animals, they followed, by day, the scanty track they had made in the woods and slept at the foot of its trees, wooed to slumber by its ceaseless noises, during the night, until the forty or fifty miles, which separated them from the river, had been traversed. Then came the building and launching of the heavy rafts, to contain their domestic utensils, and of the light and speedy canoes for themselves, on which they were to continue their long journey to the haven of rest, accompanied slowly by their cattle driven along the river's banks. As forest and open space, trees, rocks and sandy beach, succeeded each other with tiresome monotony, and as camp-fire followed camp-fire at the close of the day, they little reckoned that they had swept by the spots where the flourishing towns of Binghamton and Oswego were, later, to stand. As they rounded the curve where the Lackawanna joins the Susquehanna at Pittston, who was the wizard of their number whose divining rod would point to the priceless diamonds beneath them and tell them that their dumb animals were treading under foot riches of far greater value to mankind than all the pearls and rubies for which the world was striving? Whose fancy amongst them all could have pictured or imagined the beautiful city of Wilkes-Barré, and the coal breakers everywhere rearing their heads into the air as though they were indeed giants issuing from their long slumber in the bowels of the earth? Which of them, as they halted for the night by the site of that busy town of Danville, and watched the smoke of their fires curling lazily into the air, could have transformed it, by any power of imagination, into the volumes of black smoke which were, later, to pour from its busy iron factories, or to have even dreamed of the iron monsters which plow our waters, as their glance, perchance, rested on their tiny canoes by the river's bank? As they exchanged greetings with the Indians in their village at Shamokin can it be that there rose up before any one of them a picture of the hideous scenes of their near future, or any foresight of their murdered sons and daughters and the blackened ruins of the homes towards which they were

Type of Costume of Early Palatines.

hastening, or did the troubled dreams of any other reveal to him the fort at Sunbury, no longer Shamokin, filled with its soldiers, and sound into his astonished ears the booming of its guns?

Down the grand stream, which was bearing them, they slowly floated until their watchful eyes caught sight of a long log cabin on its shores, where now stands the capital city of Pennsylvania, and, as they looked upon the home of John Harris, it is altogether probable they saw, for the first time in all their journey, the dwelling of a white man. Cheered by the sight on they went, until they came to where the Swatara Creek joined its waters with those of its mighty brother, and at the spot where Middletown, with its busy mills and works, now stands, our wanderers at last changed their course and entered the stream which told them they were drawing near the goal towards which they had been hastening for so many weary days. To reach this goal was but to endure a few more trials and a few more hardships, and when, in the lovely Tulpehocken region, nestling at the foot of the Blue Mountains and watered by its numerous streams, they pitched their camp for the last time—it was HOME.

And what a home, indeed, was this Tulpewihaki, or land where the turtles sang and wooed. If there be any trace of Paradise still left in this world surely it is to be found in the Tulpehocken region of Berks County. Its extent was not then limited to the two smaller townships now bearing the name, but it embraced all the county west of that part of the Schuylkill River between the city of Reading and town of Port Clinton to the north, or, to state it differently, it covered all the territory watered by the beautiful Tulpehocken stream and its many tributaries, all springing from the main Kittatinny or Blue Mountains and adjoining hills. Then its streams were filled with the finny tribe, through its forests and over its hills roamed countless animals of the hunt, and its fertile soil readily gave birth to such food as its people needed. Now its plains are covered with waving fields of golden grain, or silk-tasseled corn, with bough-laden orchards of fruit, in the midst of which stand the cheerful homes and great barns, bursting with plenty, of the descendants of those who opened it up to civilization.

### THE ABORIGINES OF THE TULPEWIHAKI.

Its aboriginal inhabitants, at that time, were members of the Delaware tribe of Indians. This great nation was divided into three principal tribes—the Unamis, or Turtle, the Unalâchtgo, or Turkey, and the Minsi (or Monseys), or Wolf. It was this latter tribe which occupied the entire eastern portion of Pennsylvania, with headquarters either at Minisink, on the Delaware River, now in Pike County, or at Shamokin, on the Susquehanna River, near the present town of Sunbury. Their great sachems, or chiefs, during the English occupation were Kekerappan, Opekasset, Taminent, Allumapees (or Sassoonan) and Teedyuscung. The Minsi tribe was itself subdivided into various clans, such as the Schuylkills, Susquehannas, Neshamines, Conestogas, Assunpinks, Rankakos, Andastakas and Shackmaxons, each with its petty chief, the names of these clans being derived from the locality which they occupied, or giving name to it. Of these the Schuylkill Indians occupied the region selected by our German immigrants for their home. At the time of their arrival the chief of the clan was Manangy, whose principal village was at Tulpehocken, and on the direct thoroughfare between the Susquehanna River and Philadelphia, which added greatly to its importance and made it a frequent stopping place for the head chiefs on their way to and from the Councils held at Philadelphia. On March 12, 1705, Manangy appeared before the Lieutenant Governor, John

Evans, with a statement that the Ganawese (or Shawanees, or Piscataways) tribe of Indians, living along the Potomac, had been greatly reduced in numbers by sickness and were desirous of settling amongst their Schuylkill brethren near Tulpehocken. As an inducement towards favorable action on the part of the authorities a guarantee was given by the Conestoga Indians, along the Susquehanna River, in Lancaster County, for their peaceful behavior. The Governor promptly gave them a kind invitation to come, only engaging that they should live peaceably upon arrival. Not only did these Shawanees pitch their wigwams beside those of the Schuylkill Indians, but they gradually spread to the west and north. In 1728 Shekallamy was appointed by the Five Nations to reside amongst them and be their Chief. This he did, making his headquarters at Shamokin, becoming the firm friend of Weiser and rendering untold service to the English. He was a most valuable man, and one of sterling character.

## CHAPTER V.

### THE SETTLEMENT.

Bavaria.

THIS was the country to which our German pilgrims came from New York Province, and these were the neighbors they found awaiting them upon their arrival. Outside of the Indian villages we have no record of previous settlements, so that, in very truth, they had taken up "vacant lands." But, with age and experience, they had learned wisdom. Their serfdom at Livingston Manor had shown them that promises were but broken reeds on which to lean, their expulsion from Schoharie had taught them that "might is right" and that the rightful gift of their Indian friends was but a shadow to them when the hand of might was reached out to grasp it. This time they tried to make their title secure at the outstart. Immediately upon arrival they entered into communication with Governor Keith and obtained permission from the lawful authorities to take up such land as they needed, with the understanding that they would make full satisfaction to the proprietor, or his agents, when the latter were ready to receive the same. During the following year, learning that an agent had been appointed with ample power to dispose of lands, they addressed the petition, previously quoted, to the Governor, stating that they were ready to purchase and asking that the sale might be consummated to give them a clear title to their homes. They left it to their English friends to satisfy the Indians for the lands they might obtain.

In this paper it will be noticed that reference is made to "fifty families more who, if they may be admitted upon the same conditions, are desirous to come and settle with us," showing that a good report of the land had already reached those remaining in Schoharie. Whilst, unfortunately, there seems to be no record extant indicating the exact time when the newcomers reached Tulpehocken, yet there can be no doubt of the Governor's approval and of their arrival in due time. Indeed, it is more than probable that, for several years after the immigration of 1723, there was a more or less constant accession to the number of the Palatines. Were any proof needed of this fact it would be evidenced in the demand of the Indians, under the leadership of Sassoonan and other chiefs, made June 5, 1728, for satisfaction to be made them on account of their lands, on the Tulpehocken, occupied by the incoming Germans.

So much has been said, and not without truth, of the kind invitations given by William Penn to the Germans to settle on his lands, and of their kind reception when they came, that we take it for granted they slept, as it were, upon beds of roses. We forget that roses have thorns. Whilst William Penn was living and his lands still unoccupied he was most anxious for settlers, but William Penn was now dead, many settlers had come and others were coming, expenses were increasing and money not flowing in so rapidly as his successors desired. Indigent newcomers were not so welcome as before, even when they desired to make their homes on lands already acquired of the Indians. But here comes a body of foreigners who deliberately squat upon territory claimed by the aborigines, putting the Proprietors to the expense of satisfying the same without much prospect of any immediate equivalent return for their expenditure. To be sure these Germans claimed that they had acted by the advice and with the consent of Sir William Keith, then Governor, but Sir William had already been deposed because his ideas and plans had not been in accord with those of the Proprietors, and the Commissioners, who alone had power to dispose of lands, claimed, on their part, that the Governor's action was illegal and without either their knowledge or consent. It was a little cloud that formed on the horizon, but it was very black and bid fair to burst over the heads of our devoted pilgrims. Under God's guidance, I believe it was only because of the well-known character of the German settlers for determination, or obstinacy if you please, which decided those in authority to avoid force and resort to peaceful means of settlement, and thus averted the storm.

It will be interesting to trace events to the satisfactory conclusion which was reached by giving a few extracts gleaned from the "Papers relating to Provincial Affairs."

On May 13, 1723, James Mitchell writes to Secretary Logan from Donegal:

"I give you to know that there is fifteen familey of Duch come from Albaney, &c are now setling upp Swattarra. I sent an account of it to the Governour & councle by Cony Thomas, & an address from the upper savens to the Governour & Councle & I have heard they are Impatient for the answer, & for me to send an express on such occasions, att my own charge, will not answer."

In the letter of Nov. 25, 1727, from James Logan to John Penn, which is taken up, to a great extent, with the division of the Province amongst Penn's heirs, he says:

"For Laetetia a Tract of very good Land was laid out at a place call'd Tulpehockin about 70 miles from Philaia, by young Rees Thomas, about 5 years since, by W$^m$ Aubrey's dirėctions, at which, tho' it could not properly or regularly be done at that time, I thought it was much better to connive than oppose it. The next year our late Govern$^r$ placed the Palatines there, whom he had invited from Albany, who will certainly hold it, on some terms or other, peaceably, by agreeing to an annual Rent or a reasonable purchase, if they can, but they are too numerous and resolute to be removed; nor, since they were placed there by what they accounted an authority would it be proper to endeavour their Dissappointm$^t$."

Pushed as the Proprietaries were for money, in their letter of April 24, 1728, to the Trustees, they say:

"And on this head we must beg leave to observe, that as within these few years there have been several persons, as well others as Palatines, that have seated themselves on Lands without purchasing them, wee think moneys, more than sufficient to pay all our Father's debts might be raised from settling with them, without the sale of any other Lands, and as wee have been informed many of these people are not in a Condition to pay the full purchase their settlements are worth, they might (if you thought propper) be granted them on their paying a less consideration and raising the quitrent in proportion, which, considering the part of the purchase money abated to be entirely lost, must not be calculated to the Common Interest, but at least at three p. cent more."

We now come, chronologically, to a meeting of the

Council held at Philadelphia, in the "Great meeting house," June 5, 1728, at which were present the Delaware Indian chiefs, who had come demanding satisfaction for their lands, especially in the Tulpehocken region, which were occupied by the whites. In response to this demand they were shown the treaty made with them ten years previously, deeding to the English " all their Lands, Islands, Woods & Waters, situate between the said two Rivers of Delaware & Susquehannah." Then come the following occurrences which we quote :

" This Deed being fully explained to the Indians in their own Language, Sassoonan & Opekasset, two of those who had executed it being present, viewed their Marks & acknowledged that it was all true, and that they had been paid for all the Lands therein mentioned; but Sassoonan said the Lands beyond these Bounds had never been paid for, that these reached no further than a few miles beyond Oley, but that their Lands on Tulpyhocken were seated by the Christians.

" Mr. Logan answered, that he understood at the Time that Deed was drawn, & ever since, that Lechay Hills or Mountains stretched away from a little below Lechay or the Forks of Delaware to those Hills on Sasquehannah that lie about ten Miles from Pextan. Mr. Farmer said, those Hills passed from Lechay a few Miles above Oley, & reached no further, & that Tulpyhocken Lands lay beyond them.

" Mr. Logan proceeded to say, that whether those Lands of Tulpyhocken were within or without the Bounds mentioned in the Deed, he well knew that the Indians some few years since were seated on them & that he with the other Commissioners, of whom Richard Hill and Isaac Norris now present at the Board were two, would never consent that any settlement should be made on Lands where the Indians are seated, that these Lands were settled wholly against their minds & even without their Knowledge.

"Sassoonan said, he could not himself believe the Christians had settled on them, till he came & with his own Eyes saw the Houses and Fields they had made there.

"Mr. Logan proceeded & said, that he was sensible the Palatines were settled there, but as he had observed before, it was without the Consent or Knowledge of any of the Commissioners, And how they came hither he should now make his Audience sensible. He said, that when he left his home this morning he did not expect this Affair would be now mentioned, but hearing after he came abroad that it was intended, being unable himself to walk, he had sent for one Paper, which he could easily direct to, that if he could have gone himself amongst his Papers, he could have produced some Letters & Affidavits that would more fully explain the matter, but he hoped that what he had there would be sufficient to make it clearly understood. It was a Petition from those Palatines themselves, directed to the late Governour, Sir William Keith & the Council, all wrote in the hand of Patrick Baird, who was then Secretary to the Governour & Clerk of the Council, & who it was that drew it would appear by its Stile."

(Here follows the petition of the Palatines to Governor Keith, previously quoted.)

"Mr. Logan observed upon this petition, that by the whole Tenour of it, as well as the Writing, 'twas very easy to judge from whom what hand it originally came. It is addressed to HIS EXCELLENCY the Governour Sir William Keith; who (as they are made to speak) OF HIS GREAT GOODNESS PERMITTED THEM to inhabit on Tulpahaca

THE PENNSYLVANIA-GERMAN SOCIETY.

Creek. His Excellency is to recommend them to the Agents, that they may have sufficient Rights and Titles made to them for such Lands as they should have occasion to buy; And to Him they apply also, that by His Authority they might be freed from the demands of the Indians. It will therefore no longer remain a question, (he said) tho' nothing more than this Petition were produced, by whose authority these foreigners had been encouraged to invade these lands to the manifest Injury of the Proprietor, and to the great abuse of the Indians, who at that very time were seated there, and had their Corn destroyed by those Peoples Creatures. And he now hoped that such of this Audience as had been so sollicitous to have the Indians complain of James Logan might go away satisfied. They had complained, and they were answered.

"Then applying to the Indians, he desired, that tho' these People had seated themselves on Tulpahockin Lands, without the Commissioners Leave or Consent, yet they would not offer them any violence, or injure them, but wait till such time as that matter could be adjusted.

"Mr. Hamilton being at the Board desired the Governours Leave to say a few words which he did to this effect.

"It was not difficult, he said, to account for the Indians mentioning at this time the affair of their Lands, considering the pains some had taken to perswade them they were wrong'd. That having accompany'd the Governour in his late Journey to Mahanatawny, with divers Persons of as good note as any of this City, on the News sent down to us forreign Indians in that neighborhood, he had heard some things very positively advanced amongst the Inhabitants concerning this Injustice to the Indians, which as he could not then believe to be true, he had wished to see them sett in a true Light, and to that purpose he thought it would be most proper for these persons in this Audience to declare openly what they had to say, that if true it may be known who are to bear the blame, or if false that they may be convinced of their Error.

"Thomas Rutter, Senr., who had been call'd on by Sassoonan, stood up & denied he had ever uttered any such thing, as that the Indians had not been satisfied for their Lands, &c.

"Mr. Logan further desired the Governours Permission to speak to another Point, which tho' proper to be taken notice of at this Treaty, yet he intended it, he said, for the sake of the Audience only.

"It was with the utmost astonishment, he said, that he first heard the Story he was about to mention, for he could scarce believe it possible that any Man could be so lost to all Sense of Shame as to form it, but he had received such numerous Accounts, & from such credible Persons of its being said & spread by many, that he could no longer forbear believing what he had so repeatedly been assured of.

"He was sensible, he said, of our present Unhappiness in having Divisions fomented amongst us. Great Pains were taken to infuse into the Minds of such as could be prevailed on, a Spirit of Contention & Faction. To divide & confuse, & by any means to perplex the Government has been the principal aim of some, the instances of it are obvious. But whatever they may do amongst ourselves, it is exceeding wicked to carry their Endeavours amongst the poor innocent Indians, & to spirit them up to uneasiness by perswading them they are wrong'd in their Lands.

"Yet if anything can be worse, it is that ridiculous, that shameless but malicious Story he rose up to speak concerning himself, vizt: That the Proprietor had sent him over a vast Quantity of Indian Goods, Strowds, & he knew not what, for a Present to the Indians, all which (they were pleased to say) he had converted to his own Use in Trade. This was a home Push against him, for perswade the Indians of this & nothing can incense them more, That this wild & wicked as it is, has been currently said, many of those who now heard him speak very well knew. It required indeed a vast Stock of Assurance to say it, but he was certain none would have so much as to own it to himself, they must deeply blush, if it were possible for such to blush to acknowledge it. It would have been a great Pleasure to him, he said, to have received anything of that kind, & he would gladly have applied it as intended, but he had been so far from making Advantages that way that his own Generosity to the Indians had cost him more than he should name. Their malice who invented & spread this Story is to be pitied, but even the Indians themselves have more sense than to believe it.

"Mr. Hill, first Commissioner of Property, delivered himself to this Purpose.

"That it was stipulated at the first Settlement of this Province, between the Proprietor William Penn & the Indians, that they should sell no Lands to private Persons or to any besides himself, or his Commissioners. And afterwards a Law was Enacted to the same Purpose, that all the Purchases made of the Indians by any other than the Proprietor or his Agents should be entirely void, which Law is still in Force. The Proprietors Commissioners, in his Absence, have ever been strictly carefull to avoid granting any Lands that were not first duly purchased of the Indians, nor would they ever suffer them to be putt off from any Lands on which they were settled, even where they had fully sold all their Rights till they would voluntarily remove. The Commissioners therefor would never have agreed to that Settlement of the Palatines on the Tulpy-hockin Lands for the Indians were then seated on them, but we see by what Methods they were disturbed. The Gentleman then at Helm, not only took upon him to order the Settlements of the Proprietors Lands, but so far to direct even in these affairs that the application must be made to him also, to be freed by HIS AUTHORITY from the Indians Demands.

"It fully appears therefore, where the sole Foundations of these Complaints lies, & how groundless all the Noise is, that has been made of the Commissioners patenting the Indians Lands. This can arise from no other than a mischievous Design to beget animosities, and raise a Disaffection in the Inhabitants, And 'tis probable, that it is with a view to possess the People with an opinion that all our Treaties with the Indians, with whom a Friendship has been so carefully cultivated from the beginning, & of which we have reaped the happy Fruits are only on Affairs of Property & the Purchase of Lands, & therefore that the Publick should bear no part of the Charge. The contrary of this fully appears at this time, And when the Proprietor or his Commissioners have occasion to treat with the Indians about those Affairs, the Publick has never been troubled with the Expense of it."

The Governor then said.

"My Friends & Brethren :

"We have now brightned the Chain & strengthned our League, & we are as one People. I have commanded all the English, by a printed Proclamation published through all the Contrey, to be kind to the Indians, which you shall hear read unto you & interpreted."

And the same was accordingly interpreted unto them, with which they appeared highly satisfied.

This brought the following reply from the Proprietaries to the Trustees, under date of Nov. 11, 1728:

"We are not without hopes that there is much more due from Palatines and others, that have settled on lands for some years Past, than will be sufficient for our Present Exigencies; and that there is also several Thousand pounds on Bond due from others, who bought Lands many years since which it is now high time to call upon for payment, & Therefore, we think it Requisite that you should give them all notice to hand in their money, allowing them some Reasonable time to provide it, and if there should be any that Cannot raise it, we think you may Justly require That they should submitt their estates to a Rent charge Equivalent to the Principal & Interest, & that such as should neglect to pay or give that satisfaction, should be Compell'd to it by Law.

"We look upon the purchasing of the Indian Claims to any of the Lands that have been, or may be settled, to be a matter of great Consequence, & therefore, we desire that you will Take the most prudent measures which occur to you to accomplish it, especially, That of Turpehockin, & what you Can Reasonably thereabout concerning which you had so great a Dispute in your Treaty with the Indians."

It was one thing, however, to direct their Trustees to compensate the Indians for their lands, and quite another thing for the Trustees to procure the means with which to do it. On Sept. 17, 1729, Secretary Logan writes: "But of all these [the Tulpehocken and Minisink Lands] there is not one acre yet purchased of the Indians, and their Purchases will certainly prove high now. Who is to bear the charge of these is not for me to determine."

Again, on Nov. 16, 1729, he tells them:

"Another great Point which must, without any Loss of

time, be resolv'd on, is to make new Purchases of the Indians, without which we may expect a war that would run this Province in the extreamest Confusion, none being worse fitted for it. I have always been scrupulously careful to suffer no settlem[ts] to be made, as far as I can prevent it, on their Claims, but S. W. Keith made the first outrageous steps in settling those Palatines at Tulpyhockin. In the meantime I have done all in my power to caress those Indians and keep them in temper, alwayes soothing them with an expectation that their brother, John Penn, their Countryman, would come over, & exactly treading his & their Father (W. Penn's steps.) would doe them Justice."

The correspondence given is sufficient to afford the reader an insight into the condition of affairs. Whilst we have seen that our German immigrants from New York Province were not especially welcome, and that, even in Pennsylvania, the shadow of another ejectment hung over them, yet it is a great pleasure to consider the comparatively honorable treatment accorded them in the latter Province. Unwelcome as they were, when the Proprietors realized that they were actually there and were disposed to do right, they, in turn, were willing to make any just terms with the strangers whereby they might obtain their long-sought homes.

Finding that the presence of one of the Proprietors was sorely needed, Thomas Penn came over in August, 1732, and started in to straighten out matters. Not only were satisfactory arrangements made, gradually, with the Palatines, enabling them to gain valid titles to their properties, but on 'September 7, 1732, a deed was obtained from the Indians, for which due compensation was given, covering the entire Schuylkill Region, including, of course, that drained by the tributary Tulpehocken Creek. Giving, as it does, the price paid for the garden spot of Pennsylvania, also the names of the Delaware Sachem, and other Indians, together with a proof of the fact that Conrad Weiser, himself, had a hand in it, the writer deems the deed of sufficient interest to give in its entirety.

## CHAPTER VI.

### Indian Deed—Sasoonan &c, 1732.

WE, Sasooaan alias Allummapis, Sachem of the Schuylkill Indians, in the Province of Pensilvania; Elalapis, Ohopamen, Pesqueetomen, Mayeemoe, Partridge, Tepakoaset alias Joe, on behalf of our Selves and all the other Indians of the said Nation, for and in Consideration of twenty brass Kettles, one Hundred Strowdwater Match coats of two Yards each, One Hundred Duffel Ditto, One Hundred Blankets, One Hundred Yards of half Thicks, Sixty linnen Shirts, Twenty Hatts, Six made Coats, twelve pair of Shoos and buckles, Thirty pair of Stockings, three Hundred pounds of Gun Powder, Six Hundred pounds of Lead, Twenty fine Guns, twelve Gun Locks, fifty Tommyhocks or hatchets, fifty planting houghs, one Hundred & twenty Knives, Sixty pair of Scissars, one Hundred Tobacco Tongs, Twenty four looking Glasses, Forty Tobacco Boxes, one Thousand Flints, five pounds of paint, Twenty four dozen of Gartering, Six dozen of Ribbon, twelve dozen of Rings, two Hundred Awl blades, one Hundred pounds of Tobacco, four Hundred Tobacco Pipes, Twenty Gallons of Rum and fifty Pounds in Money, to us in hand paid or secured to be paid by Thomas Penn, Esq', one of the Proprietors of the said Province, the receipt whereof we do hereby acknowledge, Have Granted Bargained Sold Released & Confirmed and by these presents Do Grant Bargain Sell Release and Confirm unto John Penn, the said Thomas Penn & Richard Penn, Esq", Proprietors of the said Province, all those Tracts of Land or Lands lying on or near the River Schuylkill, in the said Province, or any of the branches streams fountains or springs thereof, Eastward or Westward, and all the Lands lying in or near Swamps Marshes fens or Meadows the waters or streams of which flow into or towards the said River Schuylkill, situate lying and being between those Hills called Lechaig Hills and those called Keekachtanemin Hills, which cross the said River Schuylkill about Thirty Miles above the said Lechaig Hills, and all Land whatsoever lying within the said bounds and between the branches of Delaware River on the Eastern side of the said Land, and the branches or streams running into the River Susquehannah on the Western side of the said Land, Together with all Mines Minerals Quarries Waters Rivers Creeks Woods Timber & Trees, with all and every the Appurtenances to the hereby Granted Land and premises belonging or appertaining, To have and to Hold the said Tract or Tracts of Land Hereditaments and premises hereby Granted or mentioned or intended to be hereby Granted, (That is to say all those Lands situate lying and being on the said River Schuylkill and the branches thereof, Between the Mountains called Lechaig to the South, and the Hills or

Mountains called Keekachtanemin on the North, and between the branches of Delaware River on the East, and the waters falling into Susquehanna River on the West,) with all and every their Appurtenances, unto the said John Penn, Thomas Penn and Richard Penn, their Heirs and Assigns, To the only proper use and behoof of the said John Penn, Thomas Penn and Richard Penn, their Heirs and Assigns forever, So that neither We the said Sasoonan alias Allummapis, Elalapis, Ohopamen, Pesqueetomen, Mayeemoe, Partridge, Tepakoaset alias Joe nor our Heirs nor any other Person or Persons hereafter shall or may have or Claim any Estate Right Title or Intrest of in or to the hereby Granted Land and premises or any part thereof, But from the same shall be Excluded and forever debarred by these presents, In Witness whereof the said Sasoonan alias Allummapis, Elalapis, Ohopamen, Pesqueetomen, Mayeemoe, Partridge, Tepakoaset alias Joe have hereunto set their Hands and Seals, at Stenton, the Seventh day of September, in the year of our Lord one Thousand Seven Hundred and thirty two, and in the Sixth year of the Reign of King George the Second over Great Britain, &c.

We, the above named Sasoonan alias Allummapis, Elalapis, Ohopamen, Pesqueetomen, Mayemoe, Partridge. Tepakoasset alias Joe, Doe hereby Acknowledge to have had and Received of & from the above named Thomas Penn, all & every the above mentioned parcells & quantities of Goods and fifty Pounds in Money, being the full Consideration for all & Singular the above Granted Lands & premises, and Doe Acknowledge our Selves fully Satisfied & contented for the same, as Witness our Hands.

Sealed and Delivered by Sa-  Sasoonan als Allumapis,
soonan, Alalapis, Pesquee       his × mark.
tom, Ohopamen, Maye-     Alalapis, his × mark.
moe, Partridge & Tepakoa- Pesqueetom, his × mark.
set, in the presence of       Ohopamen, his × mark.
  James Logan,          Mayemoe, his × mark.
  Thomas Freame,        Partridge, his × mark.
  Isaac Norris, Jun$^r$,            his
  Robt. Charles,        Tepa × hoasset,
  Peter Lloyd,                mark.
  W. Plumsted,
  James Hamilton,
  Mord. Lloyd,
  James Steel.

---

Be it Remembered, that on the twelfth day of July, in the Year 1742, I, Lingahonoa, one of the Schuylkill Indians, in the Province of Pensilvania, happening not to be present when my Brethren, Parties to the above Deed, signed & executed the same, but having now received my full Share and Proportion of the several Goods & Consideration above mention'd w$^{ch}$ was left for my use in the Hands of James Logan, Esq$^r$, And having now heard the s$^d$ Deed read interpreted & explained to me, I Do hereby signify and testify my full & free Consent Agreem$^t$ & Approbation of & to the granting bargaining & selling all the above described & granted Lands, And do hereby join in the Sale & Conveyance thereof, To hold to and to the use of the above named John Penn, Thomas Penn & Richard Penn, their Heirs & Assigns forever. Witness my Hand and Seal, at Philadelphia, the s$^d$ 12$^{th}$ July, 1742.

*Indian Deed.*

Witnesses present—      The × mark of
B. Franklin,                        Lingahonoa.
Wm. Peters,
Conrad Weiser,
Lyn Ford Lardner.

Be it Remembered, that on the twenty fourth Day of September, in the Year of our Lord One Thousand Seven Hundred and Fifty Seven, Before me, William Allen, Esquire, Chief Justice of the Province of Pennsylvania, Personally appeared James Hamilton, William Plumsted and William Peters, of the City of Philadelphia, Esquires, and severally made Oath on the Holy Evangelists as follows, And first the said Deponents, James Hamilton and William Plumsted, say that on or about the Day of the Date of the within first written Deed, they saw the same Deed signed and sealed as within by the within named Sassoonan, Alalapis, Pesqueeton, Ohopamen, Mayeemoe, Partridge, and Telakoasset, in Presence of them these Deponents and the several other subscribing Witnesses thereto, and that the names James Hamilton and William Plumsted thereto subscribed to attest the same are the proper Handwriting of them these Deponents severally and respectively, And the said Deponent, William Peters, on his Oath saith, that on or about the Twelfth Day of July, in the Year of our Lord One Thousand Seven Hundred and Forty Two, he the said Deponent, William Peters, was present and saw the within written Deed Poll or Memorandum of that Date, which is subjoined or wrote under the said within written Deed of the said Sassoonan and Others, duly signed as within, and sealed by Lingahonoa, One of the Schuylkill Indians therein named, both the said Deeds having been first carefully read, interpreted and explained,

THE PENNSYLVANIA-GERMAN SOCIETY.

ANNA EVE, WIFE OF COLONEL JOHN CONRAD WEISER.

THE PENNSYLVANIA-GERMAN SOCIETY

JOHN CONRAD WEISER.

to the said Lingahonoa, before his Signing as aforesaid, in Presence of this Deponent and the other subscribing Witnesses, And that the Name William Peters subscribed as a Witness to the said Lingahonoa's Signing and Sealing the said subjoined Deed Poll or Memorandum, is the proper Handwriting of the Deponent.

Will. Allen.

Indorsed—Indeed Deed—Sasoonan, &c.—for Lands on Schuylkill. Dated 7$^{th}$ Septem$^r$, 1732. Recorded Page 114. N. B. Boileau, Sec$^y$.

Commencing the world anew under such circumstances, as our Palatines were obliged to do, is it any wonder that there was more or less disorder at their settlement, in the sense that there was no government and that every one did as he pleased. Evidently the effort was made to systematize matters, but without avail. They had not yet recovered from the first effects of their newly found freedom. Weiser pointedly remarks: " There was none among the people who could govern them; every one did as he pleased; their obstinacy, to this day (1745), has been much against them."

There were constant accessions, however, to the number of the first feeble band. In 1728 other families left Schoharie and settled there, amongst whom were:

| | |
|---|---|
| Leonard Anspach, | Caspar Hohn, |
| George Zeh, | Johannes Noecker, |
| Johan Jacob Holsteiner, | Michael Lauer, |
| Andreas Kapp, | Jacob Werner, |
| Johan Philip Schneider, | Jacob Katterman, |
| Jacob Löwengut, | Heinrich Six, |
| Philip Theis, | Conrad Scharf, |

George Schmidt.

In 1729, however, they received their most important accession when Conrad Weiser, Jr., left Schoharie with his wife and four small children, Philip, Anna Madlina, Frederick and Anna Maria, the eldest but five years of age, and settled one mile east of the present town of Womelsdorf. He was followed in the spring of 1744 by his brother, Christopher Frederick, who settled not far distant and from whom spring most of the Weiser descendants living at this time in that general vicinity. John Conrad Weiser, the father, did not migrate to Pennsylvania, but remained in residence in New York. According to one account he

*Conrad Weiser*
*Interpreter*

"piloted this small colony to Tulpehocken," but "the crowd proved too anarchal for him." Of this we have no evidence, and we do know that he never settled in Penn's Province. In the year 1746 he felt a yearning desire to see, once more, his children and grandchildren at Tulpehocken. With the assistance of Conrad he reached his son's home, but with much difficulty. He was very infirm and frail when he came and lived but a short time after, when he fell asleep in death, surrounded by his weeping descendants, at the age of 86 years. His remains are presumed to lie in the graveyard adjoining the Tulpehocken Church, but the tomb can no longer be distinguished among the many in that locality, if, indeed, it be there. So ended.

from an earthly standpoint, a fruitless life, sterling, good man as he was; one filled with toil and trouble, surrounded by danger and difficulty, and unaccompanied by present reward. The character of the elder Weiser has not been sufficiently appreciated. Descended from an honorable family, like his ancestors a "Schuldheisz," or chief magistrate of Gross-Aspach, County of Bachnang, Duchy of Wurtemberg, Germany, as well as a man of means even after the utter ruin of his home in 1693, it was but natural that he should become the leader of the mass of Palatines who were gathered at London, in 1710, for transportation to America. Instead of added honor this meant but added toil, suffering and responsibility. How well he performed his duty is now a matter of history. His stand against imposition in New York Province, his perilous visit to London for justice, his assiduous efforts to find homes for his countrymen, his patriotic service with the contingent from New York to fight the French in 1711, have all been told but too briefly. The great mistake of his life was his second marriage, in 1711, to a woman much younger than himself, by whom he had three children—John Frederick, Jacob and Rebecca. She seems to have been not only unkind herself to her step-children, but to have been instrumental in causing the father to use harshness towards them. The immediate result was that two of the sons—George Frederick and Christopher Frederick—were bound out, in 1711, with the father's consent, by the Governor of New York, to a gentleman on Long Island, and the family began to break up. His own happiness seems to have been greatly disturbed, as is evidenced by his longing to visit Pennsylvania. Like many another he was forced to look above for that peace which was denied him here below.

When Penn purchased, in 1732, from "the tawny sons

## First Settlers.

of Tulpahoca" their lands, the villages, which they occupied, clustered "north of the present site of Womelsdorf, under the Kittatiny or Blue Mountain," embracing the territory west of the Schuylkill River, as previously mentioned. Before the erection of Berks County, in 1752, the township of Tulpehocken was a recognized division, being a part of Lancaster County in 1729. Because of its great size, in 1734 another township was laid off from it and erected, called "Heidelberg" to commemorate that part of the fatherland from whence many of the settlers came. These two districts were, later, again subdivided, but such subdivisions are of no special bearing on our present paper. The early inhabitants, therefore, of the old townships of Heidelberg and Tulpehocken were composed, mainly, of the immigrants from New York Province, and their names are of especial interest to us.

Rupp names the following as amongst the first settlers:

| | |
|---|---|
| John Adam Diffebach | Peter Lebo |
| Christian Lower | Christopher Weiser |
| John Spycker | George Beistein |
| Jacob Lederman | Jacob Ketterman |
| Jacob Fisher | Peter Ansbach |
| John Soller | Michael Ried |
| Jacob Sorbert | Herman Walborn |
| Francis Wenrich | Frederick Reed |
| Ulrich Schwartz | George Landauer |
| Stephen Conrad | Henry Boyer |
| Conrad Sherf | Martin Stip |
| John Livergood | Abraham Lauch |
| Peter Sanns | Peter Serby |
| Adam Stein | Casper Reed (Ritt) |
| John Edwards | Peter Reed |

George Null
Jacob Livergood
Francis Parvin
Henry Seller
Ludowick Ansbach
George King
John Fohrer
Christopher Keiser
John Trautman
Michael Detweiler
Nicholas Kinser
John Moir
Henry Stein
Christian Moir
George Sherman
Peter Keephart
William Keyser
George Jacob Sherman
Gottfried Rohrer
Jacob Hoffman
Mathias Doebler
George Wolf
Bartel Dissinger
George Tallinger
Jacob Reed
Frederick Kaufman
Christian Frank
Rudolph Moir
Michael Kofner
George Brosius
Jacob Bortner
Jacob Casert
Casper Reed

Lenard Rees
Adam Lesh
Philip Brown
Peter Shever
Felty Unruth (Onroo)
Jacob Miller
Jacob Hubelor
Jacob Wilhelm
Jacob Bartner
Nicholas Olly
John Hovershen
Simon Scherman
John Riegel
Jacob Schwaner
Henry Millberger
Wolf Miller
George Paffinberger
George Kantrico
Daniel Moir
Martin Schell
Adam Jordan
Jacob Tantor
Jacob Fullman
Mathias Noffziger
John George Meirslem
Jacob Miller
Simon Bogenreif
Andrew Wollinbeck
George Gotyman
Henry Reidenbach
John Baltzer Shever
Valentine Brindseil
Martin Warner

*First Settlers.*

Christopher Ulrich
Johann Jacob Snebly
Mathias Bricker
John Pontius
Peter Criser
Daniel Lucas
William Keyser
Philip Gebhart
George Ulrich Fisher
William Dieler
Conrad Reber
Valentine Bungardner
Nicholas Lang
Frederick Stap
Valentine Neu
Christian Kurtz
John Ebberts
Michael Alberts
Peter Laux
Peter Krieger
John Weiser

William Brath
Gottfried Fitler
Peter Mink
Casper Stump
Mathias Wagner
Nicholas Hamber
Nicholas Miller
George Weaver
Philip Meade
John Philip Bunger
George Christ
Conrad Wirth
Thomas Kern
Mathias Shefer
John Ridnore
Jacob Stough
John George Mats
William Sassaman
Adam Rehm
John Adam Weaver
Jacob Houksvert

It is to be regretted that this list is imperfect and incomplete in various respects. The next available lists are the taxables of 1759. After the lapse of thirty years the numbers of the original settlers were more or less increased by the addition of others from below, and decreased by the removal of some of their own descendants. Therefore, whilst interesting in many ways, the lengthy later lists lose much of value in their bearing on our subject and should hardly form a part of this paper.

## CHAPTER VII.

### The Immigrant's First Aim for Church and School.

NOW that our Palatine immigrants have, at last, not only reached their destination but have been allowed to settle in peace and been put in the way of obtaining clear titles to their property, it is well to recall the fact that they came not for adventure, neither did they curse the land of they adoption by carrying with them the lust for gold, but they came to find a home and to bring with them a steadiness, an energy and a godliness of character which was to lay a solid foundation for the future of Penn's Province and bless it above all its sister Colonies or States. Aye! more than that, it was to be the leaven which, though hidden at first in the Pennsylvania loaf, was gradually to spread its influence throughout the whole country and permeate the entire Union. What, then, was the first act of these people, denounced, time and again, as "ignorant boors," because, forsooth, they spoke a tongue which their *learned* neighbors could not understand, thus necessitating the use, by themselves, naturally in a more or less imperfect manner, of their neighbors' language? It was, after having erected a house in which to worship their God, to place beside it a school house for the education of their children. Other settlers, in other colonies, had likewise built their churches, but it can hardly be affirmed that any of them, following the example of these despised Germans, made it an invariable rule to provide, at such early stage in their experience, for the education of their offspring.

This subject, as a whole and in detail, will be treated hereafter. It behooves us, therefore, to now consider, in a general way, only so much of it as may pertain to the early history of the immigrants from New York Province. Were the traveler of to-day, having taken a train at Reading, Penn'a, over the Lebanon Valley Railroad, to disembark at Sheridan Station and ramble along the Mill Creek road, due south, for half a mile, he would come to what is still a well proportioned, substantial stone structure, with a capacious cellar, half under ground, whence flows a strong and beautiful stream of clear water, having its rise here in a perennial spring. It is the Zeller homestead, erected by Heinrich Zeller, one of our New York Palatines, in 1745, as shown by an engraved headstone within the wall, always kept in good repair by the family, and now the property of his eighth lineal descendant, Mr. Monroe P. Zeller, whose modern residence is nearby and who is, himself, a cultured and talented gentleman, a graduate of Franklin and Marshall College and various musical conservatories abroad, where he is by no means unknown for his abilities in that direction. The Rev. P. C. Croll, who has wandered and gleaned amongst the "Landmarks in the Lebanon Valley," most entertainingly speaks of this building, which is so typical of the many substantial homes provided, even at this early day, by the Pennsylvania Germans of the Tulpehocken region, for themselves and their families. He tells us that " its walls are two feet thick, and laid up with many large and well-dressed stones. Its door posts, about five and a half feet high, and the lintel fully three feet long, are single sandstones, with some attempts at carved ornamentation upon them. The head stone over the door, and the slab bearing name and date, have rather elaborate figures and lines carved upon them. The door is broken into two, like ordinary stable doors, and consists of double inch boards pegged together with wooden pins. An iron catch, or staple, on the inside, soldered with lead into the stone door post, catches the heavy iron latch that closes the door. All the windows were originally but small square port holes in the wall; but three of these have since been enlarged into the size of ordinary windows, for more modern convenience. The rest remain intact. So does the building throughout. Its main floor, over the cellar, is arched below and leveled with stone and earth. A huge and quaint Queen Anne fireplace, twelve feet wide, graces the kitchen part of the house." It was not only a home but a fort, in addition, as all the early homes needed to be, and, during the horrors of the French and Indian War, nigh at hand, it frequently opened its protecting doors to fleeing neighbors.

There is an old family tradition that Christine, the wife of old Heinrich, seeing three savages prowling about the house, trying to gain admission, when all the family were absent save herself, descended into the cellar with an axe. Presently the head of the first Indian protruded through the port hole, when down came her weapon with deadly effect. Promptly dragging the body inside she called to the others, in a disguised voice, who, supposing all to be well, made similar efforts to enter and were in turn despatched.

This stone house, however, was the second building erected by Heinrich Zeller and, as a permanent residence, supplanted the temporary log house which he built in 1723, upon his first arrival, and which stood some fifty feet distant. It was in Zeller's log house, in 1727, when the number of the settlers had been sufficiently augmented to warrant them in such a proceeding, that a public meeting was held and it was resolved to erect a house for the worship of God, using it during the week for educational purposes and the gathering of the parish school. Without a pastor, or the immediate prospect of procuring one, widely separated as to their dwellings, and scanty of means as well as few in numbers, this action was certainly of a praiseworthy character. It was altogether a work of the laity. Amongst the pious men present, of prominence, were the Reith (Reed) brothers, Adam, Leonhardt and Michael, the former of whom is said to have presided. Others were Frederick and Michael Schaeffer and Christopher Lechner, who was chosen to superintend the erection of the building. George Scholl is said to have made the motion to erect the house of worship, which was unanimously carried. It is said that in the devotions conducted at this meeting Luther's famous battle-hymn, "Ein Feste Burg," was rendered. Mr. Croll, in speaking of this gathering, remarks, very appropriately, that though the hymn thus rendered by these devout men may not have approached, in excellence of rendition, to the efforts of our more modern trained chorus, yet how much more sincere and thrilling it must have been. The three Reith brothers, or, possibly, Leonhardt alone, promptly donated the land, over eight acres in all, sufficient for church, school house and burial purposes, and, under Mr. Lechner's superintendence, assisted by men and women, the first church, not only in the Tulpehocken region but in that part of the Province, was erected in five months, and dedicated in October of the same year. It was called " Zion's " church, but is now better known as " Reed's church," from the name of the family who were so active in its erection. It belonged to the Lutheran denomination, the faith of its early members. It is hardly possible that any clergyman could have been present at the dedication, but, as we know that a parochial school was in existence from the beginning, it is probable that its first teacher, Jacob Hannmer, a native of Manheim, Germany, officiated at these services.

To Rev. P. C. Croll we are again indebted for a description of this building which stood on an eminence near the present town of Stouchsburg. It consisted of hewn logs, with roof of thatch or tiles. The pews were made of the same material (logs with a hewn side for seats), while the pulpit was made of rough boards. An ordinary walnut table, 34 x 48 inches in dimension, donated by one of the Reiths, was used as altar and communion table, which identical table is still intact, the property of Aaron Snyder, Esq., a lineal descendant of the donor, living at Mt. Ætna, Berks County, Penna.

The question of obtaining a regularly ordained pastor was far more puzzling to our immigrants than the erection of their church, as it was to all the early German settlers in Pennsylvania.

Their earnest desire to hear the word of God expounded, which was to them not merely a vain repetition of empty sounds, but, in truth, the "Bread of Life," caused them to be less circumspect in their choice of a mouthpiece to give utterance to the same, and, most unfortunately though most naturally, led them into much trouble and endless confusion.

So great a scarcity was there of pastors for this suddenly but sparsely settled and remote district, that the immigrants were willing to give ear to the preaching of any one who seemed to be clothed with authority and whose teachings had even the remotest resemblance to their own Lutheran faith.

In August, 1730, John Peter Miller, a native of Oberant Lautern, of the Electoral Palatinate, and a graduate of the University of Heidelberg, arrived in Philadelphia, and there made application to the Scotch Synod for clerical ordination. Before receiving ordination a question for discussion was proposed, and, in answering it, he showed himself to be a man of rare endowments. "We gave him," says Rev. Andrews in a letter to a friend, "a question to discuss about *Justification*, and he answered it, in a whole sheet, in a very notable manner. He speaks Latin as readily as we do our vernacular tongue."[4]

Shortly after ordination Mr. Miller visited Weiser at Tulpehocken, and labored, as a minister of the Gospel, among the Germans, for several years.

About that time a religious excitement prevailed throughout the entire region; scores imbibed the sentiments promulgated by Conrad Beissel, the founder of the "German Seventh Day Baptist Association" at Ephrata.

Amongst the number of converts were Miller and Weiser, both of whom were initiated into that church, by the ordinance of baptism, in May, 1735. Weiser soon forsook

---
[4] Rupp.

the society, but Miller resorted to Ephrata, where he remained till the day of his death, September 25, 1796.[5]

In the meantime, about 1733, Casper Liebbecker had become teacher in the little parish school, as well as a lector to the congregation, or reader of sermons written by the fathers of the church. As the Beissel excitement died down and the people returned to their former faith an effort was made to secure a pastor, doubtless from abroad, at a salary of thirty pounds (Pennsylvania currency), but without avail; then, in despair, they turned to their teacher and selected Liebbecker for their minister, who occupied a newly built parsonage.

Whilst these events were transpiring on the borders of the Province, there landed in Philadelphia, on Sept. 11, 1728, by the ship Good Will, David Crocket, master, from Salinger Amt, Duchy Berg, in Unter Pfaltz, Germany, the missionary John Caspar Stoever, Sr., and John Caspar Stoever, Jr., a theological student 21 years of age. The former took up his life work in and about Spottsylvania, Va., whilst the latter labored as a missionary in Pennsylvania, throughout its entire settled portion, at a time when there was probably not a single ordained Lutheran minister in the whole Province except the Swedes at Philadelphia. In 1733 he received ordination at the hand of Pastor Schultze, and was married at the same time, whereupon he promptly resumed his labors in Lancaster and Berks Counties.

As was to be expected, the ministry of Mr. Liebbecker failed to give satisfaction to many from the mere nature of things. With the advent of Rev. Stoever as a regularly ordained clergyman of their own Lutheran faith, came the desire on the part of many to elect him as their pastor and

---

[5] Rupp.

bring to an end the temporary arrangement then existing. But, meanwhile, Mr. Liebbecker still retained a number of adherents who may have reasoned that it was but poor judgment to cast off a tried servant, one who resided in their midst and constantly attended to their wants, to take up one whose duties allowed him to give but a portion of his time to them. Be that as it may, the congregation was divided into factions and bitter was their strife, which lasted several years and is known as the "Confusion of Tulpehocken," from the title of a statement published Aug. 11, 1742, by the wardens of the party opposed to Stoever, which was attested by Conrad Weiser.

The contention became so strong between the congregations, either having their pastor or church officers, that an appeal to the law became necessary. The whole matter was argued before the nearest Justice of the Peace, Wm. Webb, of Kennett, Chester County, who was lawful attorney for John Page, of London, the proprietor of these Tulpehocken lands, under the title of "Court Baron of the Manor of Plumton," who decided in favor of the Liebbecker party, giving them exclusive rights to the church property. This interesting document, bearing date of January 22, 1735, is still kept as a relic by Mr. Franklin B. Reed, the seventh lineal descendant of the Leonhardt Reith who donated the ground.[6] It was stipulated, however, that when no regular services were held by Liebbecker, the regular pastor, Stoever, or any other preacher who would *behave* himself, might occupy the house for worship. Under these conditions, and with the approbation of his opponents, Stoever continued to preach once a month. It is said, however, that his adherents did many things calculated to annoy, and even injure, Liebbecker,

---
[6] Rev. P. C. Croll.

as on one occasion, when a log filled with powder was placed in the fireplace, but, fortunately, exploded without harming any one.

Mr. Liebbecker died in 1738, but even then the factions failed to unite and his congregation remained without a pastor. The effort to supply his place introduced a new element of discord. Conrad Weiser had meanwhile become acquainted with Count Zinzendorf, of the Moravian Church, and was so much impressed with his religious zeal and unquestioned piety as to render him, for a while, personal aid in his labors. Aware of the conditions at Zion's Church, the Count offered to supply the vacant charge with a pastor, free of expense, who should serve them until they might obtain one of their own faith from Germany. The offer was accepted and J. Philip Meurer selected, to begin his labors in September, 1742. Pending his arrival, in March, 1742, Gottleib Buettner, a young man just ordained by the Oley Synod, took temporary charge.

At once the Stoever faction denounced him as a non-Lutheran interloper, whilst the Liebbecker party accepted him as their minister. Again an appeal was made to the law and again the attorney, Mr. Webb, decided in favor of the original congregation upon the assurance of the wardens that they would hold the church in trust for a Lutheran congregation.

Upon the arrival of Meurer, unwilling to accept him as a pastor and in the firm belief that the old church was swept away from its Lutheran moorings, Mr. Stoever and his adherents withdrew, in the fall of 1742, to found a new one, which was erected about a mile west of the former edifice and named Christ Tulpehocken Church, though now generally known as the Tulpehocken Lutheran Church.

This original building was doubtless of logs. Its foundation stones can still be seen. When the corner-stone was laid in May, 1743, there was placed in it a document setting forth the principles upon which this new church should he founded, which carefully guards against their admixture with any sects and errorists, and is signed by 166 adherents. The first building was replaced, in 1786, by a substantial stone structure, which venerable edifice is still standing. By 1743, however, the Rev. Mr. Stoever had resigned his charge at this place and was succeeded by the Rev. Tobias Wagner, who was the first pastor of Christ Church.

The old congregation, under the charge of Rev. Meurer, did not flourish. More as a matter of competition with Christ Church a new stone edifice was erected in 1744, but without avail. Finally, in 1745, the Moravians having built a church of their own, some seven miles farther down the Tulpehocken, where a Moravian settlement was founded, those who were distinctly of their faith withdrew, leaving the congregation very small in numbers and barely able to maintain services. Mr. Meurer added to his unpopularity by refusing, February, 1747, to allow the pastor of Christ Church to hold funeral services in the case of a deceased member of his congregation who requested that such might be done.

With the advent of Henry Melchior Muhlenberg in America the harassed and storm-tossed immigrants were, at last, to find rest. This work was aided materially by his marriage, April 22, 1745, to Anna Maria, daughter of Conrad Weiser. Through his efforts Weiser was finally and firmly anchored to the Lutheran faith. Through the persuasive reasoning of both the remnant of Zion's congregation were, likewise, restored to the fold from which they had temporarily wandered, and were induced to elect as

THE PENNSYLVANIA-GERMAN SOCIETY.

THE OLD WEISER HOMESTEAD NEAR WOMELSDORF.
ORIGINAL HOUSE.   ADDITION BUILT 1834.
PHOTOGRAPHED FOR THE SOCIETY BY JULIUS F. SACHSE.

their pastor, in September, 1747, the Rev. J. Nicholas Kurtz, who had been just chosen, in addition, as the pastor of Christ Church. Thenceforth, for a century, the two charges were as one congregation except in the matter of a preaching place.

There only remained to decide what interest the Moravians had in the property, inasmuch as part of the means for erecting the church of 1744 had been furnished by them. A suit was brought to test the matter and a decision reached, April 26, 1755, which affirmed the claims of the Lutherans on the ground of the original intention of the donors of the land and the large majority of membership of the Lutherans at the time suit was brought.[7]

Having traced the religious experiences of our Palatine immigrants from New York Province, so far as we may, it only remains to add a word with regard to their early efforts in education. Under the adverse circumstances by which they were surrounded it might have been excusable had they postponed action in that respect. Such was never the thought or purpose of these men. The reader has already learned that their first act was the establishment of a parochial school, a place of instruction not only for the brain, but for the heart as well. He has also been given the names of its first teachers and, now, needs but to be told that upon the death of Mr. Liebbecker, in 1738, his place, as a teacher, was taken by Valentine Kraft. When the Rev. John Nicholas Kurtz became pastor of Christ Church he also taught the parish school. I have not touched upon the Tulpehocken Churches of the Reformed denomination, feeling they were not within the scope of this paper, but it is not out of place to remark that, with their advent, came also their parish school, established by direction of the Rev.

---

[7] M. L. Montgomery.

Michael Schlatter, which had an existence as early as 1752. And the existence of these schools was not a matter of a mere day's time, but they were maintained for a century, long after the establishment of public schools. It was this firm adherence to an education, something more than merely secular in character, which caused their early action, in opposition to an untried system of general public instruction, to be misconstrued, and themselves to be maligned.

## CHAPTER VIII.

### His Influence as an Agriculturist.

THE critic who reads the pages now written in eulogy of the early German settler in Pennsylvania may well advance the argument that it were but natural for the Pennsylvania-German of to-day to sound the praise of his ancestor and to ascribe to him much of the prosperity to which this Commonwealth has now attained. If he lean towards adverse criticism he may be inclined to close his eyes to the material proofs surrounding him of the truth of what has been claimed; but no one can fail to give credence to a favorable assertion made by one not of German descent, and, not only unprejudiced, but, rather, prejudiced against the Palatines. This assertion comes from the lips of Thomas Penn himself. The reader need not be reminded of the fact that the German immigrant was looked upon, at first, with disfavor. He spoke a foreign tongue; his country was not the country of the English, and his ways not their ways; he was, frequently, indigent, and, on the surface, did not indicate his real value; and there was a galling obstinacy about him which tended to widen the breach. It cannot be denied that, for a while at least, the proprietors and their commissioners were much in doubt whether the presence of the Germans in their province was at all desirable, and whether "their room would not be preferable to their company." Under such circumstances a change of opinion, on the part of the proprietor himself, must inevitably carry great weight with it, and it cannot fail to be a source of gratification to all Pennsylvania-Germans to know that, at the meeting of council held at Philadelphia, January 2, 1738 (Col. Rec., 4–315), as Thomas Penn was summing up the past and advising for the future, he made the following just assertion :

"This province has been for some years the asylum of the distressed Protestants of the Palatinate, and other parts of Germany, and I believe it may with truth be said that the present flourishing condition of it is in a great measure owing to the industry of those people; and should any discouragement divert them from coming hither, it may well be apprehended that the value of your lands will fall, and your advances to wealth be much slower; for it is not altogether the goodness of the soil, but the number and industry of the people that make a flourishing country."

Even Penn, himself, failed to realize the greatness of the truth he uttered, because he failed to analyze the real but, to him, hidden reason which actuated these "industrious" people. On the surface, he saw a body of men, women and children fleeing for asylum to his Province, and because they were useful and law-abiding he bade them welcome. Could he have read their hearts he would have known that, in all they did, they were moved thereto by one great, irresistible desire, and that was the *love of home*. It was this "love of home" which made them cling, for weary years of terrible suffering, to the Fatherland, until "home" no longer existed; it was this same longing for a "home" which then drove them, through how much hardship we already know, to a new world; it was a "home," which would be *their own home*, they demanded upon arrival and with nothing else would they be satisfied. Now that they had found this "home" they were content to abide on it and to make of it a very garden spot and horn of plenty for the entire province.

We will have occasion presently to refer to the fact that the German settlers of Pennsylvania who occupied its border lands saved the life of the province by stopping the encroachment of the savage, and future papers treating of the French and Indian War and Revolutionary War will have some astonishing facts of interest to relate, but the writer would here impress this great truth upon the reader that the present material prosperity of the great state of Pennsylvania is mainly owing to the solid foundation upon which it rests, and that this foundation was laid by the early German immigrant who came, not as an adventurer to restlessly flit about and curse the land of his adoption by constant quarrel, intrigue and general instability, but who came for a "home," with everything that word implies in its best sense, and whose descendants today, in many cases, occupy the same home and cling to it with the same tenderness.

The first step, in the preparation of a home, from a mere temporal standpoint, was that which was required of every settler, whatever his nationality, the clearing of the land and the erection of buildings. Its value, to a colony, depended upon the perfection with which the work was done by its people.

## Founding a Home. 413

Our immigrants from New York found a wilderness stretching before them, well watered, to be sure, but of no unusual fertility, uncultivated, and the home of savages. It meant labor, and labor was given unstintingly. The temporary log cabin first came into existence for an abiding place, followed, almost immediately, by an edifice to the service of God and a building for the instruction of their youth. Then came the clearing of the land, the cutting down and uprooting of trees and thickets, the gathering together and hauling away of stones, the plowing, planting and manuring of the soil, the caring for their cattle and erection of granaries, the supply of food from the stream or woods, the wearisome carriage of grain to the distant mill, the constant guard against the thieving or murdering aborigine, the spinning and weaving of their own garments, even the manufacture of their own furniture.  With the primitive utensils then in common use, but few of us can realize the enormous amount of heartbreaking and body-wrecking labor necessary for the accomplishment of even meager results. Can we wonder that only those should persevere who were indeed in earnest? Because our Germans were truly in earnest they did persevere until they have spread abroad over the entire land, supplementing their less stable brethren of other nationalities.  Before even the break of day, during the heat of the noontide sun they toiled on, and until its rays had disappeared beneath the western horizon, when darkness made work impossible, and then they sought their needed rest in slumber, but not before each little family had gathered about its altar to sing their hymns of praise and invoke the same Divine blessing upon their future undertaking which had been showered upon their past.

Other settlers have likewise toiled and struggled, but it may well be asked what other settlers can show an equal result to these Palatine immigrants within the same length of time.  Hardly had a decade of time elapsed when, on all sides, were to be seen flourishing farms, with fields of waving grain, orchards laden with fruit, and pastures filled with well-conditioned domestic animals.  The temporary log house has given place to a two-story stone structure, a most durable, commodious and comfortable home; in place of the shedding, hurriedly erected, now stands the great red barn, upon its stone base, and with its overhanging frame superstructure bursting with plenty; and everywhere are scattered the many little adjuncts of prosperity and comfort.  How well the fathers then built is evidenced by the present existence of scores of these buildings, still home-like and inviting as of old.

## CHAPTER IX.

His Influence from an Industrial Standpoint.

THE historian is generally willing to admit that the German immigrant into Penn's Province was a successful agriculturist, and, as such, useful in its upbuilding. His praise frequently stops there, and he is inclined to give most, if not all, the credit for industrial prosperity to others. If such were, indeed, the case the influence of the Germans in the upbuilding of Pennsylvania would truly be limited. That the facts are far different is too generally unknown.

Unfortunately, in that respect the scope of this paper is limited. The writer must leave to others the burden of the proof of his assertion. His work is limited to but a small part of the territory of our great Commonwealth, and, even there, he must confine himself to the deeds of the immigrants from New York Province alone. With the imperfect lists at hand of their names, and the slight knowledge we have of their individual acts at that early date, there can be given but a few instances of the industrial activity of the race at that time. Even these will serve to show that the New York Palatines were, by no means, inferior to their brethren in such matters.

The Stiegel Mansion at Manheim. The south wall is still standing.

When we speak of industries, in this connection, such industries are meant, of course, as were practicable in that locality and at that time. These were the saw and gristmills and tanneries, besides the ordinary occupation of the smith, carpenter, wheel-wright, etc. Were we to find the Germans industriously occupied in those directions alone we might well consider our case proven. How much more so when we see them branching out in other and unexpected directions. Though the several names, to which we have especial reference, in this latter remark, are those of immigrants who came up into the Tulpehocken region from below, and not down from New York, yet their work was amongst and so identified with that of the others that this paper would be incomplete without some slight notice, at least, of them.

Stiegel's Office in Manheim. Still standing.

Baron Henry William Stiegel was one who originated a large number of industries, creditable alike to himself, his race and the Province. About 1758 he came to Lancaster County where he purchased land and laid out the present town of Manheim, according to a plan of the city of Mannheim, Germany, which he brought with him, and which is supposed to have been his native place.

Early Lutheran Church, built in 1770, on land donated by Stiegel, at Manheim.

He also built the Elizabeth Furnace, which he named after his wife. Then, to introduce a new industry and furnish labor for the inhabitants of his new town, the Baron erected extensive glassworks at Manheim. These works, he says in one of his letters, brought him an annual income of £5000. His Elizabeth Furnace was located some six miles from Schaefferstown, Lebanon County, and it was at this place he made iron stoves bearing the quaint inscription:

"Baron Stiegel ist der Mann
Der die Ofen machen Kann."
(Baron Stiegel is the man
Who to make an oven can.)

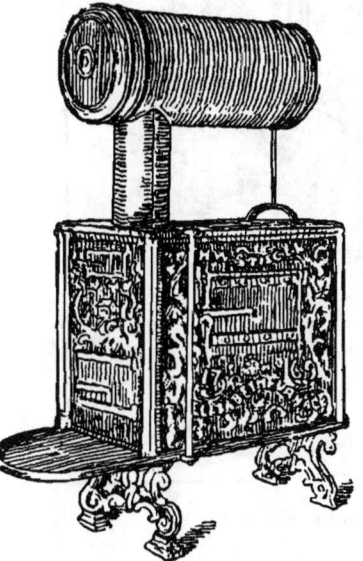

A Stiegel Ten-plate.

Stiegel Relics in Danner's Museum.

## The Stiegel Mansion.

It was not a very classical rhyme, but was easily remembered by the people, and served its purpose as an advertisement. Here also he built a summer residence. His regular home was a magnificent mansion at Manheim, built of brick imported from Germany. The house still stands but has been entirely modernized and changed in appearance. We are told there was a chapel in it where he conducted Divine worship for those in his employ. The internal arrangements, the wainscoting, the cornices, the fine piece of tapestry on the walls of the parlor representing scenes in falconry, and the beautiful tiles adorning the fireplace, were all in excellent taste and would be admired by good judges of to-day. Everything tended to show that he was a gentleman of culture and refinement. His great mistake was that he sought to get rich too suddenly. Not satisfied with his present estate he purchased the entire interest of the

Stiegel's Clock.

Messrs. Stedman in the Manheim tract, and might even have brought this venture to a successful issue had it not been for the conflict which broke out between England and her American Colonies, and which wrecked all his enterprises, making him, almost literally, a pauper.[8]

Stiegel Relics.

Another prominent example of German thrift and enterprise, in this locality, was George Ege, closely connected

---

[8] Penna. Magazine, Vol. I.—Rev. J. H. Dubbs, D.D.

with Baron Stiegel through marriage relations. He was one of the largest land owners of his time in Berks County and prominently identified with its iron industries for half a century. The Charming Forge, or Tulpehocken Forge, erected by John George Nikoll, a hammersmith, and Michael Miller, in 1749, on the Tulpehocken Creek, several miles north of Womelsdorf, also Germans, after passing through several hands, became the property of Baron Stiegel in 1763. Upon the failure of the latter it came into the possession of Mr. Ege, with four thousand acres of land, who, by 1804, had become the owner, in

School-House where Stiegel taught School in 1778, still standing.

Glassware manufactured by Stiegel at Manheim. The Table is a falling top, one of Stiegel's.

addition, of Reading Furnace, south of Robesonia, with six thousand acres, of Schuylkill Forge, with six housand acres, and of four large farms in Tulpehocken and Heidelberg townships, embracing one thousand acres, which were named respectively, "Spring," "Sheaff," "Leiss" and "Richards," the three latter after old families of the vicinity. During the Revolutionary War he was an ardent patriot and in 1783 a member of the General Assembly of Pennsylvania. In 1791 he was appointed one of the first Associate Judges for Berks County, under the Constitution of 1790, and served, with marked ability, for a period of twenty-eight years when he retired to care for his extensive business. He died, Dec. 14, 1829, aged eighty-one years, nine months, at his home at Charming Forge. His remains were interred in the cemetery at Womelsdorf.[9]

Still more closely connected with the work of our industrious immigrants from New York Province is the old mill-homestead of the Rev. Johann Casper Stoever, of whom we have had occasion to speak already. It still stands to-day, on the banks of the Quittapahilla Creek, about two and a half miles west of Lebanon, a venerable landmark of the olden times. This building, which is a large and substantial stone mill structure—originally provided with a suite of domestic apartments, and occupied by this pioneer of Lutheranism as the permanent abode of himself and family for a period of forty years—was erected in the years 1737-40. It is of so strong and substantial a character that three years were required to complete it. Considering the times and meagre facilities for building then existing, it is a massive structure—about 40 by 60 feet—with walls three feet thick, most of them as solid to-day as when first erected, though composed of simple, undressed surface stones, many of them no larger than a man's fist. No penknife has yet been found strong enough to break the cohesiveness of the mortar which binds them together firm as cement. For more than a century and a half the waters of the Quittapahilla have here turned the machinery that has ground out the one kind of grist for the customer and the other for its owner. That it did not do its work in vain for him who first built it is evidenced by

---

[9] M. L. Montgomery.

the fact that, at his death, Mr. Stoever was the possessor, besides this mill property, of over five hundred acres of the richest land in the valley.[10]

In glancing at the German industries of the neighborhood where our immigrants did their life work, with all of which some of them were identified, we dare not overlook the paper mill at Ephrata, where Conrad Beissel established his cloister in 1733. The mill furnished not only paper for the ordinary avenues of trade, but it especially supplied paper for the printing press there established about 1745, the third in the Province, and the first to print both English and German. From its office issued many tracts and hymns, together with several large works in which the views of the founders were fully explained. Its " Martyr's Mirror," printed for the Mennonites in 1748, a volume of some fifteen hundred pages, has been considered by competent authorities, in view of the facilities then existing, to be relatively as impossible and venturesome an undertaking as would be the issue of a new encyclopedia by a modern printing house. It was the first biographical work in Pennsylvania. When Congress left Philadelphia, and, for safety, met at Lancaster and York, the Continental money was printed at Ephrata. It is to be regretted that many of the books have been lost and destroyed. Just after the battle of Germantown three wagon loads of books, *in sheets*, were seized and taken away for *cartridges*. They were the unbound sheets of the " Martyr's Mirror," which General Washington directed to be removed to prevent so large a stock of paper from falling into the hands of the enemy.

Of the German immigrants whom we know to have formed a part of those who came from New York Province,

---

[10] Rev. P. C. Croll.

or whose parents were of the number, we are not entirely without record of some who took an active part in furthering the industrial prosperity of the Province, besides the large number who, in a more humble capacity, were its unnamed weavers, tailors, carpenters, builders, rope makers, blacksmiths and wheelwrights.

We are told that a mill existed in Tulpehocken settlement in 1732, as, in October of that year, the provincial treasurer paid £1 5s. to the *miller of Tulpehocken* for ten bushels of meal delivered to Sassoonan. The Reed and Lechner families, who had intermarried, seem to have been the most prominent in the establishment of industries. They and their descendants were instrumental at different times, in the erection of a mill, in Marion, for making cement; a grist mill near the junction of the Millbach with the Tulpehocken, nearly opposite to the site of which came, later, a carding mill; a carding mill and an oil mill a short distance up the Millbach, erected by Christopher Lechner after 1776; a saw mill, which, in more recent years, took the place of the oil mill, and new grist and clover mills which supplemented the old wool-carding mill, both the work of the Lechners.

Indian Girl. Primitive Corn Mill.

An interesting incident in the lives of these two families occurred in 1793, when General Washington visited the grave of Conrad Weiser. He requested the presence of his former comrades-in-arms, Christopher Lechner and the Reith brothers, Jacob and Valentine, who hastened to comply and spent several hours in the company of their great commander. The patriotic heroes lie buried in the graveyard of the old Reed Church, their graves being marked by sandstones, the inscriptions on which have become almost obliterated. Jacob Rieth died in 1821 and Valentine Rieth in 1825, aged, respectively, seventy-five and seventy-six years.

South of Stouchsburg, on the Tulpehocken, was a clover mill put up by Peter Sheetz, its site being occupied by a grist mill erected by Adam Klopp.

Somewhere in the township, its exact location not given, was a tannery conducted by Johannes Miller.[11]

And so, with patient research, the list might be and will be enlarged, with more or less interest to the reader, until it has reached much greater proportions than the respectable showings already made. The main purpose at this time, however, is to produce such an amount of historical data as may be conclusive evidence that the German settler in Penn's Province was greatly instrumental in its present prosperity, not only as a mere agriculturist, but in the fundamental work accomplished by him in the rearing of varied and substantial industries, and that here again those who came from New York were not derelict in their duty.

---

[11] M. L. Montgomery.

## CHAPTER X.

### The Pennsylvania-German Patriot.

INSTRUMENTAL as was the Pennsylvania-German in the founding and upbuilding of our Commonwealth, because of his value from an agricultural and industrial standpoint, yet, in a still greater degree, were his sterling qualities manifested when, as a patriot, he braved, unflinchingly, the onset of the savage, and never permitted the Indian to cross the border lands which he inhabited. It was at the cost of his home, his property, the lives of those he loved, even his own life, that the "lower counties" were enabled to pursue the usual avocations of their life in peace, and to prosper, unmolested. No one then thought of finding fault with German stubbornness and conservatism. Had it not been for this stubbornness at that time, and for the sacrifices which the Germans made, the advance of civilization in Pennsylvania would have been delayed for half a century. In all these events the immigrants from New York Province were especially prominent.

It is an unfortunate fact that the occurrences of the French and Indian War in the Province of Pennsylvania have not received the attention which their importance demands. To such an extent is this true that the casual reader is frequently under the impression that its settlers were spared the trials and dangers experienced by others, and would be appalled to learn the true condition of affairs. Whilst a future paper will give, in detail, the noble part taken by the Germans in this struggle, yet this writing would be incomplete without, at least, some slight reference to the doings of the New York immigrants.

To many it might seem strange that, at any time, there should have been an outbreak amongst the Indians in a Province whose Proprietors made every effort to deal with them fairly and honorably. Various reasons for it might be advanced, but, after all, they resolve themselves back to the old story of human weakness inherent in both the red and white man alike. In the first place, with good intentions on the part of the government, the Indian was not invariably treated with fairness. He never forgot the "Walking Purchase" of 1737, in Northampton County; he could not fail to realize, eventually, how meanly insignificant were the trinkets he received in exchange for his vast tracts of rich territory, even though they were the price which he himself asked for them; nor could he dismiss from his memory the many instances in which he was ill-treated and defrauded by individual settlers. On the other hand, the aborigine, who was a savage, did not and could not possess such a fine sense of honor as to cause him to willingly give up his hunting grounds, for which he had been paid his own price. When his whiskey was drunk, his matchcoat worn out, his fish-hooks and cheap muskets broken, and his squaw was tired of her beads and mirrors, then he remembered the lands which were no longer his own, and only awaited his opportunity to regain them and to be revenged upon those who occupied them in his stead.

This opportunity came to him when the Frenchman, dreaming of a vast power in the New World and the annihilation of his English foe, plied his mouth with strong drink whilst he whispered honeyed words of temptation into his ear until his brain teemed with the thoughts of what might be, and, with savage cunning, he only awaited developments to make up his mind with whom he should cast his lot. In the summer of 1755 the settlers of Penn's Province were sleeping over a loaded mine, and little recked that the torch was already lighted which should scatter its sparks all about them and fire it.

It seems difficult to realize that this culmination of affairs found the Province utterly unprepared, and without forts, soldiers or arms with which to defend its people. Warnings had been given in vain, and the dangers of the future fully laid bare, but the constant disagreement between the Proprietors, as represented by their Governor, and the Assembly, prevented any action from being taken. In 1740 an appeal was made to the King, explaining the condition of affairs, and begging that the Province might be placed in a proper state of defense before it would be too late. The discussion was kept up until 1744 but had no result, as the Assembly constantly claimed that there was no need of it. What availed it if some hundreds of German lives were lost and some hundreds of their homes destroyed so long as a few hundred or thousand pounds sterling were unexpended.

The defeat of Braddock, in July, 1755, and apparent superiority of the French arms, finally determined the

## Indian Massacres. 429

wavering redskin to cast in his lot with the foe and take up the hatchet against the English. In October came the massacre at Penn's Creek, on the West Branch of the Susquehanna, and by November the savage swarmed along the Tulpehocken region of the Blue Mountains. The first blow fell on the immigrants from New York Province and their children, and the foresight of those who had placed them on the frontier, avowedly as a barrier against just such an outbreak, was apparent. Well for the Province

Trials of German Settlers.

was it that these men had come to their new homes through much tribulation; that they had already been hardened to war, its terrors and alarms; and that they were so conservative and old-fashioned as to be willing to make many sacrifices to retain the homes they had gained with so much labor.

No sooner had the news of the Indian murders up the Susquehanna reached the ears of Conrad Weiser than he immediately alarmed the neighborhood. The farmers at once gathered together, armed with guns, swords, axes or pitchforks, whatever they chanced to possess, until some two hundred had rendezvoused at the house of Benjamin Spicker, near Stouchsburg. Then, whilst they stood with bared heads, Mr. Kurtz, the Lutheran clergyman who resided nearby, exhorted them to do faithfully the duty which lay before them, and invoked the Divine protection upon them. After Weiser had divided them into companies of thirty men, each of which selected its own commanding officer, they took up their march towards the Susquehanna, having first despatched a party of fifty men to occupy the Swatara Gap in the Blue Mountains and close that gateway to the enemy.

It is not for us, at this time, to tell how their numbers increased rapidly on the way, nor to follow them in their experiences. We may only add that it soon became apparent that their services would be needed at home much more than at the distant point towards which they were moving, and they accordingly retraced their steps.

It was none too soon they did so. The appalling nature of the great danger which threatened the Province was now evident to all, and the Government was awaking to a realization of its duty. Hasty arrangements were made to organize a Provincial regiment; Conrad Weiser was promptly commissioned as Lieutenant-Colonel in command of the First Battalion, and immediately ordered to report at Philadelphia for consultation as to the best methods of defense.

During his brief absence on this duty the savages burst the barriers of the mountains, not yet defended, and began

## Conrad Weiser's Account.

their merciless butchery. We will let Col. Weiser tell the story in his own words, as we find them in his report of November 19, 1755, to Governor Morris, as follows:

"Honoured Sir:

On my Return from Philadelphia I met in the township of Amity in Berks County, the first news of our cruel Enemy having invaded the Country this Side of the Blue Mountain, to witt, Bethel and Tulpenhacon. I left the Papers as they were in the Messengers Hands, and hasted to Reading, where the Alarm and Confusion was very great. I was obliged to stay that Night and part of the next Day, to witt, the 17th of this Instant, and sot out for Heidleberg, where I arrived that Evening. Soon after, my sons Philip and Frederick arrived from the Persuit of the Indians, and gave me the following Relation, to witt, that on Saturday last about 4 of the Clock, in the Afternoon, as some men from Tulpenhacon were going to Dietrich Six's Place under the Hill on Shamokin Road to be on the watch appointed there, they were fired upon by the Indians but none hurt nor killed. (Our People were but Six in Number, the rest being behind.) Upon which our People ran towards the Watch-house which was about one-half a mile off, and the Indians persued them, and Killed and Scalped several of them. A bold, Stout Indian came up with one Christopher Ury, who turned about and shot the Indian right throught his Breast. The Indian dropt down Dead, but was dragged out of the way by his own Companions. (He was found next day and scalped by our People.) The Indians devided themselves in two Parties. Some came this Way to meet the Rest that was going to the Watch, and killed some of them, so that six of our men were killed that Day, and a few wounded.

The Night following the Enemy attacked the House of Thos. Bower, on Swatara Creek. They came to the House in the Dark night, and one of them put his Fire-Arm through the window and shot a Shoemaker (that was at Work) dead upon the spot. The People being extremely Surprised at this Sudden attack, defended themselves by firing out of the windows at the Indians. The Fire alarmed a neighbor who came with two or three more men; they fired by the way and made a great noise, scared the Indians away from Bower's House, after they had set fire to it, but by Thomas Bower's Deligence and Conduct was timely put out again, so Thos. Bower, with his Family, went off that night to his Neighbour, Daniel Schneider, who came to his assistance. By 8 of ye clock Parties came up from Tulpenhacon & Heidelberg. The first Party saw four Indians running off. They had some Prisoners whom they scalped immediately, three children lay scalped yet alive, one died since, the other two are like to do well. Another Party found a woman just expired, with a male Child on her side, both killed and Scalped. The Woman lay upon her Face, my son Frederick turned her about to see who she might have been and to his and his Companions Surprize they found a Babe of about 14 Days old under her, raped up in a little Cushion, his nose quite flat, which was set right by Frederick, and life was yet in it, and recovered again. Our People came up with two Parties of Indians that Day, but they hardly got sight of them. The Indians Ran off Immediately. Either our People did not care to fight them if they could avoid it, or (which is most likely) the Indians were alarmed first by the loud noise of our People coming, because no order was observed. Upon the whole, there is about 15 killed of our People, Including Men, Women and Children, and the

Enemy not beat but scared off. Several Houses and Barns are Burned; I have no true account how many. We are in a Dismal Situation, some of this murder has been committed in Tulpenhacon Township. The People left their Plantation to within 6 or 7 miles from my House against another attack.

Guns and Ammunition is very much needed here, my Sons have been obliged to part with most of that, that was sent up for the use of the Indians. I pray your Honour will be pleased, if it lies in your Power, to send us up a Quantity upon any Condition. I must stand my Ground or my neighbours will all go away, and leave their Habitations to be destroyed by the Enemy or our own People. This is enough of such melancholy Account for this Time. I beg leave to Conclude, who am

Sir
Your very obedient
CONRAD WEISER.

Heidleberg, in Berks
County, November 19th, 1755,

P. S.—I am creditably informed just now that one Wolf, a Single man, killed an Indian the same Time when Ury killed the Other, but the body is not found yet. The Poor Young Man since died of his Wound through his Belly.

To Governour Morris.   (Penn. Arch. 2, 503.)

It will be noticed that the names given in this sad recital are, so far as known, all those of families which emigrated from New York Province. What they there experienced was but the beginning of similar horrors, to extend over some years of time, but their relation is sufficient for our present purpose.

It has been shown that the settlers were already making

such arrangements for their safety as could be carried out. Watch towers and garrisoned block houses were established at various points. By this time, however, the Government had decided upon establishing a chain of forts along the entire Blue Range. , One of the first of these to be erected, and the largest of the series, was Fort Henry, which was situated near the base of the Round Top Hill, three miles north of Millersburg, in Bethel Township, Berks County, on the farm of Dietrich Six, where the people had located the watch tower mentioned in Weiser's letter. Standing, as it did, on the top of the rising ground, it had a most commanding view of the entire valley.

Fort Henry stood nearly midway between the other two defences erected by the Provincial authorities on the territory settled, in any part, by the German immigrants from New York. Fourteen miles to the West of it was placed Fort Swatara, close to the Gap of the same name in the mountains, and eleven miles east of it was located Fort Northkill, right at the foot of the Blue Range, about two miles north of Strausstown, in Upper Tulpehocken Township, Berks County. The cellar of the latter is still visible, although the winds of a century and a-half have almost completely filled it with the leaves of the forest.

These forts, with all the others between the Delaware and Susquehanna Rivers along the Blue Mountains, were garrisoned by details from Colonel Weiser's Battalion of the Pennsylvania Regiment, most of whom were of German blood. It is reserved for another to tell of their deeds, to relate the horrors with which they were surrounded and to show how their brave and energetic commander, in spite of his advanced years, was chiefly instrumental in bringing, once more, peace to his unhappy countrymen and quiet to the distracted Province which had become his adopted home. It is enough, for the present, to have shown that those who had fled from the persecutions which they suffered in New York Province were not unmindful of the debt of gratitude owing to the Province of Penn which had received them in such different manner.

It would be but an act of poor justice to our New York immigrants and their descendants were we to leave the reader to suppose that their service to Pennsylvania came to an end, even from a military standpoint, with their actions during the French and Indian war. When the oppression of the Mother Country toward her colonies became intolerable, and the effort to gain freedom was unavoidable; when, at last, the clash of arms came, and an army must be gathered together, the first troops to reach Washington, in front of Boston, were Pennsylvanians from the German border counties, and the first of these Pennsylvanians was Captain Nagle's company, from Berks county, which arrived, in advance, on July 18, 1775.

When, in God's providence, years later, He saw fit to make every human being in our glorious country free and equal, and, in His wisdom, saw fit to bring about this result through the horrors of a great Civil War, when brother was arrayed against brother, and father against child, again the German citizen of Pennsylvania stood up, manfully, for the right, and again was he foremost in the performance of duty. The first company in the Union to respond to the call of the President for troops was from Berks county, the Ringgold Light Artillery, who volunteered on April 16, 1861, and in whose ranks were not only many Pennsylvania-Germans, but, better still, no small proportion of those who were descended from the Palatines who wended their way, with much toil, from New York Province, to found a home, after many trials and tribulations, in Pennsylvania.

## CHAPTER XI.

### The Founding of Towns and Cities.

FROM their very nature and training the majority of the German immigrants were inclined to devote themselves to the pursuit of agriculture and the establishment of various industries. Indeed, settling as they did in what was practically a wilderness, no other course of life lay open to them. Their influence in the upbuilding of Pennsylvania, therefore, was especially evident in those directions. They were a band of God-fearing and worshipping, patriotic men, who were satisfied to patiently toil in the laying of a solid, substantial substructure, so that when, eventually, the house should be reared upon it there could be no question as to its endurance. It would, truly, be "founded on a rock."

Yet, whilst not, in one sense, men of the city, it would be an injustice to them were we not to call attention to the fact that they, too, had a hand in the establishment of communities in the Province. Without dwelling upon the

## Sale of Lands. 437

numerous beautiful and flourishing towns, in and adjoining the Tulpehocken region where settled our New York immigrants, and with the origin of which they, or their descendants, were closely identified, such as Wernersville, Robesonia, Womelsdorf, Sheridan, Myerstown, Lebanon, Stouchsburg, Strausstown, Millersburg, Rehrersburg, it is well to remember that some of their number, amongst them especially Conrad Weiser, were instrumental in giving a most substantial start to what is now the great city of Reading, with its 85,000 inhabitants and hundreds of diversified manufacturing establishments.

The first thought of the Proprietors of the Province was to remunerate themselves and enhance the value of their property by the sale of land. With this in view on February 19, 1733, a tract of 1,150 acres was surveyed and disposed of to Richard Hockley, covering what is now, approximately, North Reading; on March 19, 1733, there was surveyed a tract of 300 acres for Thomas Lawrence, patented October 27, 1733, and on April 22, 1738, a further tract of 137½ acres was surveyed for the same person and patented February 16, 1739, both taking up practically the present center of the city; on February 19, 1733, a tract of 150 acres was surveyed for Samuel Finney, in the present southern part of Reading. Some years after these grants had been made the Penns conceived the idea of laying out a town at that locality, and made an effort to re-purchase the ground. The Hockley tract was considered to be best adapted for the purpose, but its distance from the ford, which was opposite the Lawrence property, militated against it; then again, on the Hockley land, water was not so abundant near the surface, whilst on the Lawrence and Finney properties fine springs bubbled up at many places. So soon as the owners of the Lawrence and Finney tracts were aware of the desire of the Proprietors they refused to sell, and it was not until the Penns had commenced laying out lots on the Hockley land and they began to realize their mistake in holding out too long, that, on December 30, 1745, the Lawrence tracts were conveyed to Thomas Jenkins and gradually found their way into the hands of their original owners, on March 6, 1748.

During the fall of 1748 a town was laid out on the Lawrence land, and named "Reading" after the county town of Berkshire, in England, the home of the Proprietors. At this time there was not a town or village in the adjoining territory, though the population was about ten thousand. The nearest town was Lebanon, twenty-eight miles to the west, which was laid out in 1740.

Three prominent representative men were appointed as commissioners for the purpose of making a prompt sale of the lots laid out. They were Conrad Weiser, Francis Parvin and William Hartley. Publication of the proposed sale was made and on June 15, 1749, the conditions of the sale were read to a large number of people. They were briefly as follows:

1. Every whole lot of sixty feet was to be subject to a ground-rent of seven shillings, payable to the proprietaries; to begin on March 1, 1750.

2. Lots on the great square (Penn Square) were to be built upon with brick or stone in one year from March 1, 1750.

3. Lots on Main (Penn) Street, not on the square, were to be built upon in two years.

4. Other lots within blocks adjoining Main Street were to be built upon in three years.

5. Lots in blocks remote from Main Street were to be built upon in five years.

6. A sixty-feet lot, if too large, should be divided and ground-rent apportioned.

7. All who should take lots before March 1, 1750, were licensed to take stones for building purposes from any land of the proprietaries, assigned by Hartley.

8. Title would be made upon erection of building; and no assignment could be made before erection of building.

9. Privileges of ground-rent at seven shillings to continue only to March 1, 1750.

10. Houses should be built according to the regulation of the streets.

11. Persons might thereafter apply to the three commissioners named in reference to lots.

12. Two whole lots would be allotted in some convenient place for building houses of religious worship.

13. Persons who should intend to take lots were to send in their names and the time in which they could build, but they were not to undertake to build sooner than they really could, otherwise they might obstruct the progress and success of the town.

Town lots were, doubtless, sold at once and, probably, buildings erected speedily. It seems, however, that no patents were taken up until 1751, as this is the first record given, and is as follows:

1751—seven lots

| Lot | Patentee | Lot | Patentee |
|---|---|---|---|
| 2 | Conrad Weiser (Justice) | 34 | Conrad Weiser |
| 11 | Daniel Steinmetz (merchant of Philadelphia) | 106 | Adam Witman (shop and innkeeper) |
| 29 | Isaac Levan (Exeter, Yeoman) | 114 | Isaac Levan |
| | | 120 | Conrad Weiser. |

In 1752 one hundred and thirty-three lots were taken, in 1753 eighty-four, and in 1754 seventeen lots, which would indicate, in 1755, a town of some two hundred dwellings and one thousand inhabitants. Mr. Daniel B. Keim gives for 1751 a total of 130 dwelling houses, besides stables and other buildings, containing 106 families and 378 inhabitants.[12]

Hardly had this thriving village, destined to become such a flourishing city, sprung into existence, when its German citizens, in accordance with the rule of their lives, took steps to provide for their spiritual and educational wants. Here again Conrad Weiser, of the German Palatines from New York Province, with others of his fellow-countrymen, was prominently identified with the progress of events. So early as 1751 the Lutherans, under the leadership of Rev. Tobias Wagner, organized a congregation. In 1752 application was made by Conrad Weiser and Abraham Brosius, Trustees of the congregation, for lots on which to erect a church at what is now Sixth and Washington Streets, the deed for which was finally executed and recorded in 1754, the consideration money being "five shillings, lawful money of Pennsylvania," together with an annual ground-rent of "seven shillings sterling money of Great Britain," dating from 1752. In the spring of 1752 a church building was begun on this ground, which was completed in 1753 and dedicated to the service of the Triune God on Trinity Sunday, June 17, 1753, receiving the name of "The Holy Trinity Church." On this occasion was presented a dedicatory poem, or hymn, composed by Conrad Weiser, of remarkable excellence both in sentiment and form. It consists of thirteen verses, of which we give a translation of the two first made by Thomas C. Zimmerman, Esq., of Reading:

---

[12] I am mainly indebted for facts as to Reading to Montgomery's "History of Berks."

"Jehovah, Lord and Mighty One!
Hear, Thou, our childlike calls;
To all who stand before Thy face
Within these sacred walls,
Incline, dear Lord, Thy gracious ear.
Nor cast aside our fervent prayer,
For sake of Thy dear name.

"The people of Thy covenant
Now consecrate this place;
Reveal, O Lord, from out the cloud
The splendors of Thy face,
That it may flood this house with light,
And banish evil from our sight,
For sake of Thy dear name."

This first church was a log building, one story, with galleries on three sides, north, west and south. On the north gallery stood the organ, whilst to the east was the chancel and pulpit. It had a steeple with a clock and two bells. This edifice gave place in 1794 to a building started in 1791 and still standing, which, for size, beauty of style and proportions, as well as stateliness and adaptability to the purpose intended, remains to this day unequalled in this part of the Commonwealth. It is of brick and large enough to contain two thousand persons, the whole number, approximately, of the inhabitants of Reading at that time. The name of its architect, unfortunately, is not known, but its magnificent steeple, over two hundred feet in height, erected in 1833, was the work of its own members, the building committee being George Boyer, John Bickel and Anthony Bickel, and the constructors Conrad Henry, William Henry and Joseph Henry. The beauty of this graceful spire remains unexcelled even at the present day.

Almost coincident with the organization of Trinity Congregation was the establishment of a parochial school and the erection of a school building. No records are extant to show the exact date when it was started, but the church minutes of 1759 refer to it as something by no means new. At that time the pastor, Rev. B. M. Hausihl, also served as the teacher. It was probably a log building situate near the church. In 1763 a lot was purchased on the southwest corner of Sixth and Washington Streets, upon which, shortly after, a most substantial one story stone schoolbuilding was placed, the parochial school transferred to it and instruction kept up continually for over a century. This structure was not finally demolished until 1894.

The German Reformed element was equally active with their Lutheran brethren in religious matters. Through the aid and influence of Conrad Weiser they obtained title, in 1754, to ground at Sixth and Washington Streets, just opposite Trinity Lutheran Church and to the east. It is supposed that a small log church was erected at that time, but in 1761 a substantial stone building was put up and in it the congregation worshipped until it was torn down in 1832 to make place for the present commodious and handsome (remodeled) edifice.

They too established a parochial school, for which a brick building was placed on ground at Seventh and Washington Streets, purchased in 1776.

From these two parent congregations have branched out many others, which, in turn, have established additional missions. Their work has not ceased at home, but has extended in all directions and has been felt in every part of the world. The good accomplished is incalculable. It has been seen that Conrad Weiser, a German immigrant from New York Province, was a leading spirit in all this work, just as he was a leader in all the events of his time, and as his father before him was a leader amongst his oppressed countrymen in New York. Others of those included within the scope of this paper aided him in his praiseworthy efforts, and, with him, were instrumental in bringing about the results which followed.

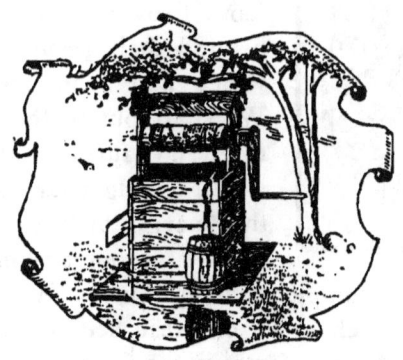

"ALL'S WELL THAT ENDS WELL."

## CHAPTER XII.

### Some Closing Reflections.

BUT it is not our duty to follow the fortunes of the German immigrants from New York Province into Pennsylvania beyond their assured settlement, which has been now set forth. We shall pursue the facts, therefore, no further in narrative, whilst asking your indulgence to that margin of truths which must always accompany mere facts to set them forth in complete intelligibility. We should know something of the character of these settlers, something as to their importance as a factor in the Commonwealth. The general testimony as to the Palatine migration is that it was made up of "quiet and industrious" people. It sought the land for carrying on agriculture, and did not largely linger in the cities. Even in such case, it followed trades and was thrifty. It was religious and desired the ministrations of God's word, which, however, in the absence of a regular ministry exposed it to the schemes and frauds of runaway schoolmasters and smooth-tongued adventurers and often resulted in suspicion and subsequent irreligion. It proved susceptible, in some degree, to the mystical element as represented by the various sects; indeed, it brought much of that element with it, but in the main it was true to that type of Christian faith represented in Arndt's True Christianity, which was its main commentary and exponent of the Gospel. Its persecutions at home and in New York had made it somewhat restive and suspicious of civil and ecclesiastical authority, to its own hurt and to the profit of demagogues. These same fears prevented an efficient church organization, favored independent congregationalism, tended toward an inordinate cherishing of their native German tongue and a sturdy resistance against the inevitable transition to English as the generations descended, which in its turn alienated those who did become English in their speech, separated them from the ancestral mass, and resulted in that disdain which some of those cherish for "Pennsylvania-German" who have hardly a drop of blood in them which is not inherited from that very source. While the numbers which came from New York were small, their testimony as to treatment there, and their witness to the bright contrast of their experience in Pennsylvania led to the choice of this latter province by almost all subsequent German migrations. Even if landed in New York, Germans at once sought Pennsylvania; and if possible, sailed directly for Philadelphia. Hence Pennsylvania became emphatically a German colony. The Bible was printed here in German; newspapers, almanacs, religious books were printed, published, sold and read in German. Attempts to force the Anglicizing of this great body failed; and we know how slowly the transition in speech has taken place even unto this day, despite the tremendous influence of English pub-

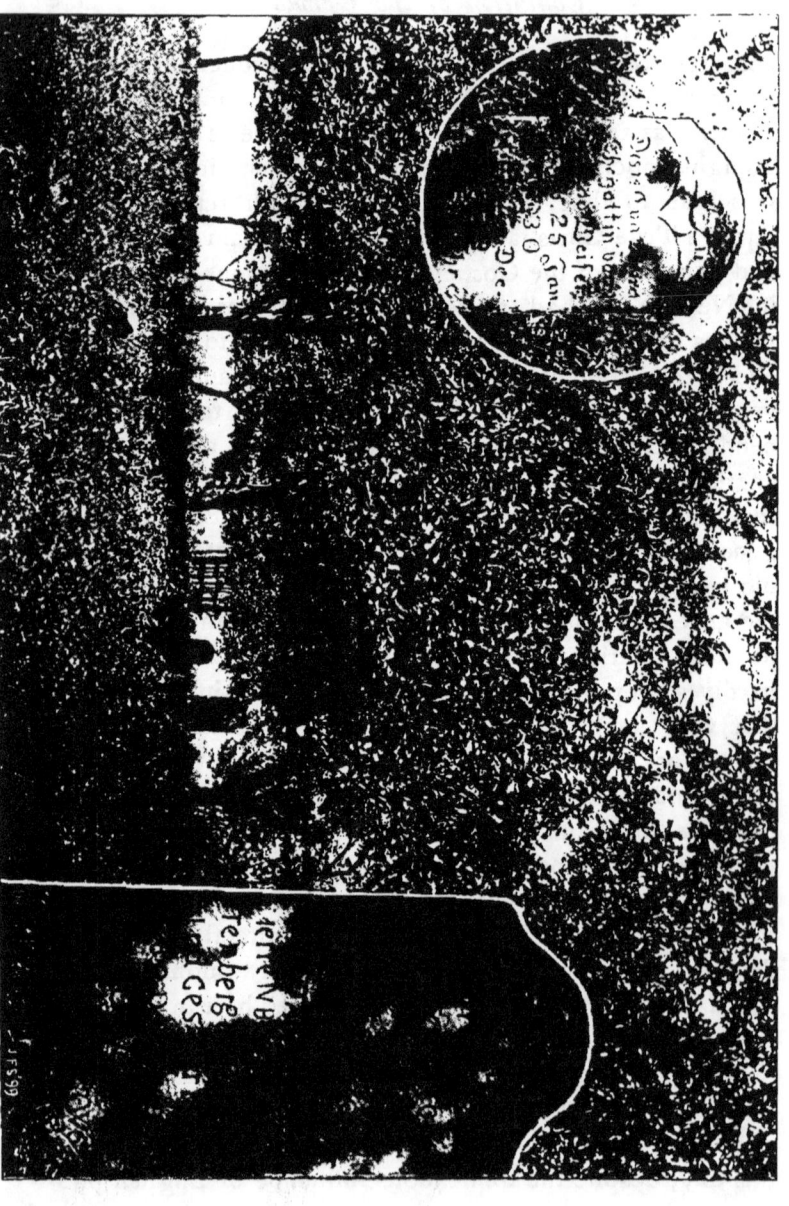

BURIAL PLOT ON THE WEISER FARM NEAR WOMELSDORF.
SHOWING THE GRAVES AND TOMBSTONES OF CONRAD WEISER AND EVA ANNA, HIS WIFE.

lic schools, the use of English in legal and business affairs, and the flood of English daily newspapers pouring over all the country side. That our State is what she is, that her influence has been which it has been, that her attitude in national crises has been praiseworthy, conservative and approved by the outcome, can never be lauded and magnified without implying a just tribute to the Pennsylvania-German.

The Pennsylvania-German has tended more to the useful element than the brilliant; it has done the work rather than achieved widespread reputation. As an example of this characteristic take the case of Conrad Weiser! We hear much of the blessed policy of equitable and peaceful dealings with the Indians under the Penn's government. But it was this Palatine immigrant from the New York Province, Conrad Weiser, who was the interpreter and agent, the one man trusted by Indian and white man, who managed this affair from 1732 until physical decay and old age, in 1760, made it no longer possible. Yet the few hear of Weiser and many laud the Penns, who had practically very little part in it, except the good sense to trust Weiser and let him manage the Indians and pay his reasonable bills for expenses and services. It was the fault neither of Weiser nor the Penns that the French and Indian War broke out; it was to the praise of Weiser that the province felt its fury no more than it did, much as it suffered from this fierce struggle. Conrad Weiser had been for eight months during his youth a member of the family of Quagnant, a Mohawk chief, was recognized by the "Six Nations" as an adopted member, had served as interpreter and adjudicator almost from that very time—his seventeenth year. What a power this man had for good or for evil! He made it a power for the good of man and for the glory of God.

He was interested in the spiritual welfare of his Indian brethren, for he was a man sincerely spiritual himself. It was largely he who made possible and efficient the missionary efforts of Spangenberg and Zeisberger, whom he accompanied in 1738 in their journeys, as he did Zinzendorf in 1742. He taught the missionaries the Mohawk language; he was their shield, their propitiating herald, their frequent companion. His toils, dangers, exposures were little less than theirs; yet who has heard of Weiser when these missionary efforts are recounted? In 1743 Weiser became acquainted with Henry Melchior Muhlenberg, the first representative and authorized missionary of the Lutheran Church. In 1745 he gave his daughter in marriage to Muhlenberg, and his influence was exerted subsequently in furthering the interests of that orderly and orthodox Lutheranism which Muhlenberg and his coadjutors in the Synod of Pennsylvania and adjacent States represented. When we read of the confusion preceding this period we ask ourselves once more, what if Weiser's influence had been against instead of for the struggling efforts of the faithful few to gather into safe folds the spiritual sheep all astray, to expose and expel knaves and imposters, errorists and ungodly ministers?

But let this suffice! After the manner of our fathers, we will not erect monuments to ourselves. We can wait until others " rise up to call us blessed." Yet meanwhile let us in filial gratitude, as in a household gathering, recount and recall the facts and the truths which prove our honorable descent, and enkindle within our own souls the high resolve to act well our part, to deserve well of our fellow-men and to be thankful for that strain of blood which should make this the easier for us to perform.

www.ingramcontent.com/pod-product-compliance
Lightning Source LLC
Chambersburg PA
CBHW061959220426
43662CB00011B/1741